# FAITH, HOPE, NO CHARITY

# FAITH, HOPE, NO CHARITY

## An Inside Look
## At the Born Again Movement
## In Canada and the United States

Judith Haiven

Foreword by Charles Templeton

New Star Books
Vancouver, Canada

First printing September 1984
1   2   3   4   5   88   87   86   85   84

Several chapters of this book have appeared in part or in whole in the
following publications: The Canadian Churchman, United Church Observer,
The Toronto Star, Quill & Quire, Maclean's, The Canadian School Executive,
Goodwin's. Chapter 11, "Good and Conscientious Employees," was the
subject of a CBC-TV documentary produced by the author for the program
Edmonton File.

**Canadian Cataloguing in Publication Data**

Haiven, Judith, 1951-
Faith, hope, no charity

Bibliography: p.
ISBN 0-919573-32-0 (bound).—ISBN
0-919573-33-9 (pbk.)

1. Evangelistic work—United States.
2. Evangelistic work—Canada. 3. Mass media
in religion—United States. I. Title.
BV3773.H34 1984    269'.2'0973    C84-091385-0

The publisher is grateful to the Canada Council for assistance
provided through the Writing and Publication Section.

Production coordinated by Jill Gibson

Printed and bound in Canada

New Star Books Ltd.
2504 York Avenue
Vancouver, B.C.
Canada V6K 1E3

# Contents

# Foreword
## by Charles Templeton

I have had considerable experience with evangelists. Over the years I have known many of them, some the most eminent in their field. Most of them were ignorant men with narrow minds and circumscribed interests. Among them are rogues and saints, charlatans and do-gooders. Most are strong on emotion and weak in logic. A few (notable among them, Billy Graham) are honourable men. The majority were raised in Christian homes and took in fundamentalist tenets with their mother's milk. A minority came later to the "born-again" experience and are sometimes a little more zealous for it. Some are earnest souls who avoid "worldliness" and material rewards with a passion akin to masochism. Others (including many of the more successful) are sexually randy, consumed by pride and dominated by avarice.

The old-time itinerant evangelist is gone and in his place we have the new electronic evangelist. It is not merely his medium which is new; he has a new message. That message is not, however, the gospel of the New Testament, but is a 20th century Christian heresy, in which a pious pablum is offered in a form that renders the teachings of Jesus unrecognizable. It is part show-business, part superstition, part pious claptrap and as unlike New Testament Christianity as is a newspaper horoscope.

With exceptions, the electronic evangelist bears little or no resemblance to his pre-television predecessors. His sanctuary is a rented auditorium or television studio. His pulpit is a TV screen. Your pew is an easy chair in your livingroom. Your only contact is with a fleeting image—a two dimensional man of God who offers forgiveness of sins, answers to prayer, instant happiness, financial security and miracles of healing, delivering none of them.

Television Christianity is an undemanding faith, a mediapostasy that tells listeners that all they have to do to be a Christian is to "believe." There are, of course, certain costs, most of them monetary, and the television evangelist reserves his most persuasive words for the financial appeal. It, and the subsequent flood of begging letters, is the electronic version of the collection plate which, having been passed, is passed forever and ever, Amen.

The offerings (mulcted mostly from the poor, the elderly and lonely middle-aged women) amount to many millions of dollars annually. Few of these dollars are used to give succor to the needy, to put food in empty bellies or to help the helpless and dispossessed. Seldom is any of the money returned to the community from which it comes. Most of it is used to buy more broadcast time, to build larger broadcast studios and to provide generous salaries, opulent homes and expensive perks for the preacher.

Nor are some electronic evangelists content to build only a "spiritual" ministry; they lust for temporal power. Jesus rejected a move to make him a king ("My Kingdom is not of this world") but that minority which vaingloriously describes itself as a "Moral Majority" covets power—political power, here and now. They seek to influence elections. They pressure legislators. They angle for invitations to the White House. And they have made it clear that, if they cannot achieve their goals of political and social change, they will themselves seek to ascend to the seats of the mighty.

These are potentially dangerous men, for, like all zealots, they are intolerant of those who do not accept their premises.

They "get their orders from God," thus, to oppose them is to oppose Him. They do not believe in freedom, and in positions of power would forbid others the right to follow their own convictions. History bears ample record that the Church in power tends to be a tyrannizing institution.

Perhaps the most objectionable of the electronic evangelists are the so-called "healing evangelists." Most of them are patently kooks, so odd that one watches them with the awed fascination usually reserved for the freaks in county fairs.

Most of today's electronic healing evangelists are much like old-fashioned "medicine men"; they live off the fears and hopes of simple people. They are quacks practising spiritual medicine without a license; offering remedies they neither understand nor have bothered to examine. They are not bright enough to be truly evil, but are nonetheless wicked men, leaving behind them a pathetic trail of emotional wreckage and illnesses sometimes worsened by neglect.

Judy Haiven has done a valuable service by examining some of these men and their methods, and some of the people who follow them. Among them are a few essentially decent fellows (men like David Mainse and Ken Campbell) who, though misguided (and in Campbell's case, occasionally bigoted) bring a degree of comfort with their truncated gospel, and a lively though small hope. Her book will help outsiders understand the world of contemporary fundamentalists, a world to which they have been introduced by their television sets. She grinds no axe and exhibits a remarkable objectivity, dealing surprisingly charitably with some of her subjects. But there is sinew in her reporting, and a toughness of mind that enables her to see beyond the facade of respectability and good intention. She sees with open eyes, unlike many men and women who find themselves unwilling to exercise the normal critical faculty when examining the religious.

The world Judy Haiven enters in this book is a circumscribed world, a world in which there is more superstition than belief. It is a world in which the Bible and

God are centre and circumference and the Devil and Demons are very real. It is an incredibly simplistic world, often irrational and given to sloganistic patness. There is among modern fundamentalists an almost delusional ability to disregard the obvious and to accept dogma regardless of the facts. They are part of the Christian subculture which, in its fundamentalist form, is flourishing. Nor is their faith difficult to understand. Ours is a dangerous and apocalyptic world, dazzling and confusing with its acceleration of information and its phenomenal technical advances. With little that any individual can do to influence the arms race and the despoiling of the environment, the increase in crime and terrorism, and the widespread abandonment of traditional morality, it is tempting to throw up one's hands and fall back in the arms of an eternal and immutable deity. And it is rewarding. It permits feelings of superiority in the guise of humility: "The rest of the world is going to Hell in a handbasket, and we alone are right."

Turning to religion is not new, of course. The difference today is that the fundamentalists are not as they were in the first half of this century, "The Lord's despised few." There are among their number many men and women of eminence, power and wealth. Their leaders use the mass media (especially television) with considerable skill and much daring. And while the audiences for their largest televised shows are nowhere near in number the extravagant claims made for them, they are sizable.

One regrets that most evangelicals no longer take Jesus seriously. Their Johnny-one-note emphasis on "being born again" and the general lack of emphasis on serving one's fellows has created Christians more interested in "giving their testimony" than in giving of themselves. Modern fundamentalism is an exclusive club, paranoid, distrustful of outsiders and much given in their worship to self-centred, self-congratulatory, elitist talk about the individual's personal relationship with God.

But for all the growth of the fundamentalist wing of the

Christian Church, it is, for all its claims, of little influence on the day-to-day life of the world. Any newspaper is testimony to the failure of the church to influence the world it lives in. Ours is no longer a Christian society, no matter how much that term be stretched. One can go for months without ever meeting a "fundamentalist" or seeing evidence of any altering of the fabric of the society by his or her ideals. We are not, as is loudly trumpeted, on the verge of a great revival.

Charles Templeton
Toronto, Ontario
July 1984

# Acknowledgements

For every interview or meeting with the subjects of this book, I came to rely on assistance from many helpful people. Many supplied background information, others gave a fresh perspective and others, still, argued with me most eloquently. To all of you who devoted time to assist me, thank you.

Many people encouraged me to research and write this book, including Professor Roger Hutchinson of the Department of Religious Studies, University of Toronto; Rev. James G. Endicott; and Jerrold Hames, editor of the *Canadian Churchman*.

For their suggestions and comments, I also thank Professor Gregory Baum; Rabbi W. Gunther Plaut; Bob Rae, MPP and leader of the Ontario New Democratic Party; Dr. John H. Berthrong, Division of World Outreach, Interfaith Dialogue, the United Church of Canada; Rabbi Reuben Slonim; journalist June Callwood; Tom Harpur, author and journalist; Alan Sheffman, Director of Human Rights of B'nai B'rith in Toronto, and Lanny Morey at the CRTC in Ottawa. A special thanks to Harvey McKinnon of Oxfam who gave me volumes of useful printed material. Caroline Walker, who first edited this book, was of great assistance.

My research and travelling in the U.S. were made easier by the assistance of the following people. Bev and Stan Hainer in Virginia Beach, Virginia; Dawn Chase Desmond of the *Richmond News-Leader*; Dick Gilbert of the Institute for Applied Economics in New York; Ira Glasser, Executive Director of the American Civil Liberties Union in New York; Charles Young in Trenton and Princeton, New Jersey; Charles E. Swann, author and theologian in Richmond; Jeremy Rifkin, author and futurist in Washington, D.C.; Jim Wallace of Sojourners, also in Washington; Jean Horstmann, now in Belfast; Ronn E. Nichols, Director of Media Services for the Congressional Black Caucus in Washington, who gave me good advice; and Bill Keller, a reporter for *Congressional Quarterly*, who was very kind. I also appreciate the time given by Gary Jarmin of the "Christian Voice" in Washington; Ned Vanhamm, Ethel Steadman and Jackie Mitchum at the Christian Broadcasting Network in Virginia Beach.

Thanks also go to Rev. Leslie Tarr, Carolyn Logan, Diane Hayward, Ken Campbell, Bruce Wood, Barbara Proctor, Peter Tabuns, Danny Goldstick, Bob Davis, John Sewell, Bob Spencer, Larry Colle, Sister Mary Jo Leddy, Paul Weinberg, Arlene Perly, Don Sawatsky and Peter Raymont—all of Toronto.

I also wish to thank the Ontario Arts Council.

In Edmonton, June Sheppard, Carol Murray, Lois Sweet and Ellen Ticoll were of great assistance. Julian Sher, writer and broadcaster in Montreal, was a good friend and made some valuable suggestions. Dr. Blair Shaw of Halifax and Kay Gordon of Glad Tidings Missionary Society in Vancouver spent hours on the phone with me.

My editor, Lanny Beckman, made many useful suggestions. Wendy Switzer improved the manuscript each time she proofread it. And my husband, Larry, always encouraging me—was the greatest help.

# Introduction

What really started me on the path to writing this book was a comment made to me six years ago.

I was president of the board of directors of a newly organized housing cooperative in the east end of Toronto. Most of the co-op members were enthusiastic about taking control over this part of their lives, in becoming their own landlord. That's except for a handful of newly born-again Christians who, increasingly, attacked the leaders of the co-op (myself and other non-born agains) for dedication to a "socialistic" principle.

In the midst of this fracas I broke my back in a sports accident. Until the doctors operated, I was paralysed from the waist down. I spent four months recovering in the hospital.

On my first day home, the leader of the born-again fellowship watched me hobble up the front steps on crutches. I didn't feel her staring at me and I was startled when she said, "Do you know why you broke your back? Because God is punishing you."

I considered for a second. "Why couldn't he just have stolen my wallet?" I joked.

"Because God doesn't steal," she replied matter-of-factly, and walked away.

As it turned out, the friction with the born agains dissipated shortly afterward when most of them decided it was time to move out of the co-op.

But my curiosity was aroused. As a so-called "secular humanist," I had been aware of a resurgence in evangelicalism in the United States and watched the television preachers with some amusement. As a Jew, I had continually heard the born agains refer to my fellow Jews as "God's Chosen People." I was surprised when then-Israeli Premier Menachem Begin awarded Jerry Falwell, leader of the Moral Majority in the U.S. and multi-millionaire TV evangelist, Israel's coveted Jabotinsky Medal, for his contribution to Zionism.

So, as a journalist, it was with fascination and some trepidation that I began to devote a good portion of my freelance writing to articles on the born-again movement.

*Faith, Hope, No Charity* is a collection of vignettes that are real life. Real life for many evangelical Christians across North America today. The book zeroes in on evangelical celebrities, like Charles Colson and Jerry Falwell, and many ordinary people who could be your next door neighbours. But all of them count themselves among the newly converted "born again" Christians.

I discovered a common thread that runs through each chapter and unites all the born agains—a type of intolerance. Anyone who is not born again, or a potential convert, is ignored at best and denounced at worst. Though they claim their charity begins at home, more often than not it stays right in their own backyards, among their own. I have met many born agains—both famous and common people. What struck me about the vast majority is that beyond the initial friendliness there is a barrier as hard as steel to those who are not of their thinking. Like members of most fundamentalist sectors of any religion or of cults, there is a "we versus them" mentality. They are holy warriors locked in deadly battle and their Christian charity is carefully preserved.

The biggest stumbling block to useful evangelical church outreach projects is what the born agains contemptuously call "secular humanism," as manifest in the liberal churches' kow-towing to atheists and socialists who believe in a "man-centred universe" where God is not in control over every aspect of man's life.

The born-again Christians I interviewed believe that secular humanism is creeping into every aspect of our lives and is destroying them.

They are worried that God is not prayed to in the classroom every day; they are concerned that ethics, morals and family issues discussed in the public school classrooms don't reflect the word of God which is clear in the Bible; they feel that most great literature—from Shakespeare to Margaret Laurence—should be either expurgated or excepted from school libraries and course curricula if the books reflect secular humanism. "We want to show the world the way we want them to see it," one teacher in a Christian day school told me, "not the way it is."

In the larger picture, the world is headed for Armageddon, just as the Book of Revelation in the Bible warns. According to most born-again believers, nuclear weapons are the last ways left for the civilized western world to show the godless Communists who is really boss.

The title of this book, *Faith, Hope, No Charity*, makes reference to the famous "commandment" in Paul's letter to the Corinthians, found in I Corinthians, Chapter 13. In his "Hymn of Love," Paul enjoined them to put the spiritual gift of "love" or "charity" above faith and hope.

The word that Paul used was the Greek "agape"—a word difficult to translate into English because it is broader than what we know as "charity" (that is: strictly giving alms to the poor) and better defined than "love." Though there are many ideas on the meaning of "love," many Christians take it to mean an abiding regard for their fellow man, a commitment to fight wrongs and injustice.

It is at this important point that the mainline churches and the evangelical church part company. Though usually the born agains insist on a literal interpretation of the Bible, one exception seems to be on the subject of faith, hope and love. In Paul's letter he insists that even if a Christian has faith, can move mountains, or gives all his possessions to the poor, or has the gift of prophecy, he gains nothing unless he has love for his fellow man.

But the born agains are mysteriously silent on love or charity. The most important issue to the born agains is their devotion to their faith—their personal relationship with Jesus Christ. Secondly, many spoke to me of their fundamental belief in Bible prophecy—as interpreted by the modern day evangelical prophet Hal Lindsey in his bestselling books. When I asked them about love, or charity, most defined it only within the narrow confines of their families, or at best their ministries. They were skeptical of and angered by the mainline churches' aid to developing countries, their speaking out on Canadian social issues, and their allying their church and their membership with popular struggles against oppressive regimes in, for example, South Africa or El Salvador.

On the other hand, for the last 20 years the mainline church has taken a radically new interpretation of Paul's message to heart. From the Catholic priest who serves as a cabinet minister in Nicaragua to the Council of Canadian Bishops who created a storm by criticizing our government's economic policies which create hardship and suffering, to the United and Anglican churches which co-sponsored the Cold Lake to Edmonton anti-cruise Easter March 1983, Canadian churches are determined to combat injustice even if it means indirectly helping people take up arms against oppressive governments.

I came to write this book from my own commitment to social activism and change. As a Jew, I was raised to believe I had an obligation to the society I live in. Over the years, that commitment has led me to help organize the communities in which I lived, contribute to the Canadian union movement, and to pursue the path of investigative journalism.

By writing *Faith, Hope, No Charity* I wanted to find out what is at the core of the rebirth of the evangelical movement in Canada and in the U.S., who is behind it and how extensive is its influence.

I travelled with a busload of 100 Huntley Street "partners" to the "Washington for Jesus" rally in April 1980. During the 14-hour bus ride, many pilgrims told me how their lives had been turned around. In Washington I was a little frightened by the forecast of 500,000 born-again demonstrators. Though only 175,000 showed up, they were treated to the frantic zeal of the evangelical heavyweights—Pat Robertson of The 700 Club, and Jim Bakker, host of The PTL Club.

A month later, I visited the headquarters of the Christian Broadcasting Network (CBN) in Virginia Beach, Virginia—home of TV's The 700 Club. My tour guide took me through what she explained were the most modern broadcasting facilities in the United States. CBN has nearly reached its goal of becoming the fourth largest network in the U.S. The 700 Club, CBN's biggest drawing card, boasts a 90-minute-a-day "talk show" format and features born-again politicians, entertainers and businessmen who discuss everything from Biblical interpretations to current events and show business. And it pays.

Their plans for the near future include 24-hour-a-day "Christian alternative" programming including situation comedies, soap operas—one tentatively named "The Inner Light"—news casts and children's shows.

But as far as my guide was concerned, personal testimony and conversion are the aim of Christian television. "I used to be a 'secular humanist' just like you," said Ethel Steadman, CBN's Public Relations Officer, in what became an all-too-common refrain. "Then I accepted Jesus as my personal Lord and Saviour and I quit working for the local newspaper and am devoting my life to Him."

In the fall, my odyssey into the heart of the born-again movement took me to Lynchburg, Virginia, Jerry Falwell's hometown. Falwell's empire totes up a modest $56 million a year take from TV viewers of The Old Time Gospel Hour and Falwell's hundreds of radio broadcasts and public appearances. His hometown holdings include a shopping centre which features a bar (though he disparages the use of alcohol), elementary and secondary schools, his Liberty Baptist College and of course his shrine, Thomas Road Baptist Church.

I first met Jerry Falwell four days after the 1980 U.S. election in dreary downtown Trenton, N.J.

Standing on the steps of the state legislature at his "I Love America Rally," winged by half a dozen Liberty Baptist Singers in thin ballroom dresses, shivering in the cold, he taunted the people in the counter-demonstration. "God created Adam and Eve, not Adam and Steve," he shouted, ridiculing a couple of men wearing sandwich boards which called for gay rights. When two reporters dared to comment on his intolerance, he told them in no uncertain terms that they had better "step in line" or they'd find themselves out of jobs.

I returned home to news that Ken Campbell, a fundamentalist preacher in Milton, Ontario, had declared holy war on the homosexual community of Toronto. In a series of full-page newspaper advertisements, Campbell and his small band called Renaissance International lashed out at members of Toronto City Council and at School Trustees who didn't measure up to Renaissance's moral standards. Campbell helped defeat Toronto's reformist mayor, John Sewell, because he dared support minority rights, which included those of the gay population.

The Canadian televangelist David Mainse of 100 Huntley Street collected thousands of signatures on a petition to the CRTC (Canadian Radio-television and Telecommunications Commission) to license a religious broadcasting station in Canada. Though his application was denied the first time around, the CRTC set up a commission of enquiry to look at the question of religious broadcasting.

While the mainline churches worry about their financial difficulties and the high cost of maintaining often aged buildings that are used once or twice a week, the televangelists are taking in millions of dollars each year, with which they buy airtime, produce often sophisticated shows and keep on top of their faith partners by mailing them dozens of fundraising appeals year in and year out.

"What is going on?" I asked myself more than once.

Religion and politics are growing closer together. The secular world is continually getting knocked by the born agains. Religion is no longer a private belief system fuelled at Sunday morning services and propelled through the weekdays by good intentions and obligation.

That kind of religion refers adherents to the mainline church. What is at the heart of the private and personal religion that comes into the living room via the television fostered by the electronic church?

Martin E. Marty, theologian-historian at the University of Chicago, differentiates between the more secular religion of the college-educated and the private and more inward faith held by people who watch the electronic church. The college-educated, he says, "will take a little dab of the Judaism they were brought up with, a little bit of Catholicism from their wife, a bit of Zen Buddhism they got in college, a weekend of est, a half-baked belief in astrology, a love for jogging, and a macrobiotic diet and kind of make up a religion out of it . . . In a way that's not recognized, that's what's happening in these programs, too [the electronic churches]. You take a little bit of one kind of belief in the Bible, another kind of belief in the Holy Spirit, another kind of borrowing of a psychological technique of motivation, another technique from sales, and you put it together but you are in control."

This book examines the people behind the television personalities and the people who believe in them.

In every chapter I've taken a unique aspect in the world of the born-again Christians—from what makes a Christian book a bestseller, to a disturbing expedition to a Christian day school, to the chilling story of a teenager who attended a hockey camp with a difference.

This book presents the human side of a movement that has been described by many as being myopic, intolerant, right-wing, fascist, even anti-Semitic; a movement which some critics view as being more a cult than a religion. One fact which unites many thinking critics is the concern that while the mainline churches appear to be on the wane, the television ministries and the born-again movement are gaining new ground.

This book is not meant to be a definitive study of the born-again movement or a cross-section of their opinions and beliefs. Rather, it zeroes in on individuals—famous and average people—who at this time are part of a revival movement.

In many cases throughout the book, I have used pseudonymns instead of people's real names. In some cases, "rank and file" members within the born-again movement asked that their names not be used. Because it did not seem important to disclose any of these people's identities, I have consistently protected them. However, I have not embellished or changed any other details of these people's experiences, lifestyle, beliefs and locations. I present them exactly as they are.

In the case of leaders, spokesmen, officials, and people publicly identified with the movement or critical of it, I used their real names throughout the book.

J. H.
July 19, 1984
Edmonton, Alberta

# 1
## Washington for Jesus

The kindly face of 100 Huntley Street's host David Mainse flickered on the television screen. "When one million concerned Christians gather at the nation's capital April 29, 1980, only God knows what will happen," he read from a leaflet. He stared into the audience, "One Nation under God, can it become a reality? Of course it can and it will. And we Canadians are going to help make it come true." It was billed a National Day of Humiliation, Fasting and Prayer for all Christian Americans.

"100 Huntley Street is hiring a bus and we have room for 60 people who feel it's their calling to help their good neighbours from south of the border turn their country back to God. So if any of you viewers want to help, please call the switchboard and reserve your seat on the bus that's taking us to Washington for Jesus."

I phoned to book my ticket immediately. Ninety-five dollars guaranteed me a seat on the bus and two nights' accommodation in a Washington hotel. It would be a good chance to meet and talk with Huntley supporters. Also, I had heard news reports about the involvement of the evangelical movement in the 1980 U.S. presidential election race but the reports had been followed up by the media's silence. Was anything really happening? Perhaps at Washington for Jesus I would be able to find out.

Two weeks later, wrapped in two woollen sweaters and my raincoat, I waited patiently with a group of 30 outside the Huntley Street studio in downtown Toronto at dawn on a cold, wet April morning. The night watchman unlocked the doors, herded us into the dark cafeteria, flicked on the lights and announced the coffee was on him. Few of us knew one another, so we sat singly, watching the rain on the windows, some hunting for a familiar face.

The sun had poked through the clouds when David Mainse bounded into the cafeteria. "Well, well, what dedication to the Lord's work has brought you people out on such a cold and wet morning?" he said. "I'm *always* here at this time but you folks deserve a special 'Praise the Lord' from us here at the studio today! I'm not going to Washington for Jesus."

Groans and a few brave "why nots" rippled through the room.

"Well, I have the show to do. But Doug Burke is going to be your chaperone," Mainse laughed. With another "Praise the Lord," he dashed out the door.

A couple of minutes later a thin man of medium height and build, pale skin and a Jamaican accent, sat down beside me. Doug Burke (who is head of the Huntley Communications Division) wanted to get to know each of us on the trip. "When were you born again?"

"Never," I told him as quietly as I could.

"Never," he thundered, standing up.

"No, I'm Jewish. I'm here to find out what you people are going to do at the rally. I'm writing an article for the Anglican Church newspaper.

I must have lost him somewhere at the start because he called over his wife, Bunty, a red-haired woman with a benign smile. "She's one of God's Chosen People," he said, pointing to me.

"Well, Praise the Lord," Bunty said enthusiastically. "Glad to have you aboard. Have you ever met the Jews for Jesus here?" I looked stunned. "Well, anyway, they are coming by car and will meet us in Washington. Maybe I can introduce you."

Word that I was a writer got around. Of the 50 people on the trip, half asked if I'd interview them. They wanted everyone to know their personal testimony and how they came to be born again.

John and Marina sat across from me. *The Good News Bible* was open in John's lap and I noticed they held hands and prayed together for most of the trip. At a rest stop, they told me their story.

Now in their mid-30s, they had emigrated from Poland as teenagers. Both of them felt lost in their new land. John got a job immediately as an apprentice jewellery-maker. Though a Catholic, religion held very little appeal for him. After work he spent his hours in bars, picking up girls and having a good time.

Marina was raised by very strict and religious Catholic parents. She ran away from home and married John at 18. They had two boys, now in their early teens, and Marina stayed home to look after them.

But Marina had been under a lot of stress. The children were growing up without "Christian" values, misbehaving at school and even stealing from the corner store. She was desperate. One afternoon, when she was watching television, she absent-mindedly tuned into The PTL (Praise the Lord) Club. Host Jim Bakker personally appealed to her, she felt, to join his ministry by accepting Christ as her Saviour. She sent a small donation to The PTL Club so she could receive regular newsletters.

When she told John, he was angry. Angry because she did something without consulting him and angrier still because she announced her new love was for Christ. He felt alone, left out.

He began to smoke dope and drink heavily after work. When he was fired, he refused to look for a new job. He told Marina that if God really cared, He'd find a way to provide for them. Marina was heartbroken, but she continued to pray and wait for an answer. They hit rock bottom.

"It was the wee hours of a Sunday morning," John recalled. "I had just come in from shooting some pool, but I wasn't drunk. I turned on the television, glad that Marina was in bed so I didn't have to talk to her. Ernest Angley was asking people in the studio audience to come forward to commit themselves to Christ. [Ernest Angley is a U.S. evangelist and faith healer.] Suddenly, he looked straight at me and commanded me to come forward and put my hands on the television set. I felt God's presence run through me and I cried out for Marina.

"She jumped out of the bed, came running and screamed because she saw me sobbing like a baby. It was that night I dedicated my life to Christ and took him as my personal Saviour. I was born again."

Marina squeezed his hand and pointed to the open Bible. "Our luck changed. Jesus was in charge. John got the opportunity to take over another jeweller's business for a while and eventually he worked hard and got to own his own shop."

"We now own a house, a business that is thriving and much more," John told me proudly.

Now even their boys watch the evangelical TV shows. "We never miss Huntley Street or The PTL Club," Marina said. "I just praise the Lord when I think of where we were not too long ago."


I picked my way through the sleeping bodies. It was after 10:00 p.m. and few of my fellow travellers were awake. I sat down beside a young man reading a looseleaf binder. A sticker on his jacket said, "Hello, I'm Tim."

"Hi, Tim," I said.

Tim was in his late 20s, and he looked like a university graduate student. He smiled back at me, "You're the reporter, I hear. See this? This is what you should write about."

Sections of his binder were colour-coded with tabs on the dividers. "What is it?" I asked.

"Well, you might say it's a key to my life. I have a girlfriend who isn't born again. I'm having a hard time dealing with her. This binder is what they give away at the Bill Gothard seminars. [Bill Gothard is an evangelist in the U.S. Bible Belt.] I've taken all of them and they deal with how you as a Christian can deal with life."

The table of contents listed nine subject areas. How to: discern root problems; overcome self-rejection; respond to authority; conquer bitterness; overcome anger; achieve moral freedom; have purpose in life; gain financial freedom; experience genuine love.

"This," he noted, "allows you to let God live through you. It shows you that you can trust God for everything."

"Like what?"

"Well, should I marry my girlfriend or not, for instance? She doesn't believe in marriage, but I as a Christian do. The problem is what to do so she will be a Christian wife. I want my wife at home. She wants to work.

"This guide, 'How to experience genuine love,' helps me. I used to think I loved her but I don't think I do. She wants sex—I say sex only after marriage."

"You're over 21," I said.

"You know, Judy, it wouldn't matter if I was 101. God says people should remain pure before marriage and I believe in that. Otherwise, what's the difference between humans and animals?"

Tim worked as a poultry inspector for the federal Department of Agriculture in Toronto. Lately, he said, he had become restless at work and welcomed the chance to take a few days off.

"I like my work," he confided, "but it bugs me to be working for Trudeau. He's a Communist, he even held a Communist Party card. I'd rather be ministering to people and helping them more directly. I'm just waiting for Jesus to lead me where He wants me to go."

When we arrived in Washington, our Gray Coach driver took us on a brief tour. In the brilliant spring sunshine the city looked dazzling with its white pillars, stately buildings and boulevards of bright green trees. Then he dropped us at our motel, a small family-run business on the outskirts of town. The bus returned to ferry us to the various events.

My assignment from the Anglican Church newspaper entitled me to press status. I picked up my bulging kit and badge at the press trailer right in the Mall. This enabled me to interview the speakers and to sit in a roped-off area.

The press conference at the National Press building the next day was a shambles and it soon degenerated into a shouting match between Pastor John Gimenez, of Rock Church in Virginia Beach, and liberal reporters. Gimenez, credited with originating the idea of "Washington for Jesus," was joined by Jim Bakker of The PTL Club and Pat Robertson of The 700 Club. (Jerry Falwell did not participate and did not attend.)

"Tuesday, April 29, 1980 has been set apart to call God's people to repentance," said John Gimenez, at the press conference. "As we talk to congressmen and senators and other leaders in government, we found that some of the men who govern the nation are despairing. Many have lost hope for the future. Many see America today as the "helpless giant" and they see the Church as the "Sleeping Giant...

"Many urged us, as Christians, to take a stand for God, to wrest back the nation from the forces of unrighteousness. 'We are at a point in America now that it's either God or chaos and ruin,' one senator said...

"God has allowed all kinds of problems and crises to cause us to turn to Himself. About the only thing we haven't seen yet is the wrath of God upon this country, God's judgment of sin. And it is certain to come unless God's people repent—turn!—and intercede before God for the land." The press kit spelled out what we were supposed to be doing here. Repent it was.

The night before the main Washington for Jesus rally, I

had attended a Youth Rally in the 57,000-seat Robert F. Kennedy Stadium, miles from the Mall. A disappointing 30,000 "youth," ages eight to 80, sat in the open air in the cold drizzle. Entertainers like the Imperials, Nancy Honeytree, Pat Boone and Barry McGuire were there.

Washington for Jesus paid $25,000 to rent the subway which operated a shuttle service between the RFK Stadium and the Mall, where the main rally was held. The train was nicknamed "Holy Roller" by a group of born agains from Texas. "It has a good ring to it," said one. "Sorta captures the spirit."

Though the leaders expected over a million the next day, barely 175,000 showed up on the 23-block Mall, between the Capitol and the Washington Monument, among them our busload of Canadians. As marchers were lined up state by state, we had nowhere to go. We were eventually squeezed between Iowa and New York—a problem geographically—but, thanks to the oversize Canadian flag one of our troupe carried, at least we stood out. We marched in disorganized fashion along Constitution Avenue to the Washington Monument. In the brilliant sunshine and balmy spring weather, 175,000 people in front of the Capitol was still a moving sight.

More than 50 speakers—interspersed with prayers, blessings and gospel tunes sung by a thousand-voice choir—addressed the quiet and reverent crowd of mostly white Americans. The speakers ran the gamut from western entertainer Dale Evans, to Jim Bakker and singer Pat Boone, who especially prayed for the people in the entertainment industry to receive Christ. Rev. Pat Robertson, host of The 700 Club, warned, "High crime rates, accompanied by widespread dishonesty, the erosion of family life, chaos in standards of sexual behaviour and a rise of humanistic influence in public education, at the same time that Bible reading and prayer

*Top*: A rally bumper sticker. *Above*: The Canadian contingent in a circle of prayer at the Washington Mall. *Below*: Fellow travellers on the 100 Huntley Street pilgrimage to Washington for Jesus. Judith Haiven is seventh from left, second row.

*Top*: Some of the 175,000 in attendance. *Below*: A ''pro-life'' demonstrator.

have been removed from the public schools, have contributed to the breakdown of traditional American values." Many Americans I spoke to at the rally agreed.

The most energetic speaker was Rev. Arthur L. Blessitt, the "Sunset Strip Minister" from Hollywood. Since 1969, Blessitt has travelled 17,000 miles on six continents toting a 12-foot, 90-pound wooden cross on his shoulder and evangelizing. His voice boomed out across the Mall.

"God is sending a cleansing through us. He's filling us with fire, a baptism of fire. Give me a 'J'—that isn't loud enough. Give me an 'e'; give me an 's'; a 'u' and an 's'! Who is the hope of the world? Who is your Lord? Who are you gonna tell the world about? Go! Go! Go!"

Some people knelt and kissed the ground; others spoke in tongues; many raised their arms and cried "Praise God" and "Hallelujah!"

Other speakers included Ben Kinchlow (also of The 700 Club) and Bill Bright, head of the Campus Crusade for Christ, and Demos Shakarian, founder and president of the Full Gospel Businessmen's Fellowship International.

Although Gimenez specifically stated at the rally that "We are not here to influence the government," representatives of 20 religious groups, including the National Council of Churches, issued a statement charging the gathering was specifically political. The choice of Washington as a site was unquestionably seen as political.

Organizers announced in advance that the entire Congress and the presidential candidates had been invited and 535 seats made available. Just prior to the rally a list of 11 senators and 150 congressmen planning to attend was issued. Rally organizers were reported to have visited individual congressmen, including former astronaut turned U.S. Senator John Glenn.

A loose coalition of liberal and civil rights organizations denounced the rally as a covert lobby under the cloak of a prayer meeting, the prelude to campaigns to impose its brand of Christian morality on the entire nation, but they didn't specifically mention the upcoming election.

The *Guardian*, a left-wing weekly, pointed out on May 4, 1980 that the rally was the first national right-wing mobilization tying together emotional "new right" "pro-family" issues such as abortion and homosexuality with traditional right-wing platforms of increased militarism and a return to state and local power.

That night in the Sambo (sic) Restaurant next to our motel, a dozen of us in the Canadian contingent discussed the day's events.

"I guess I liked it because it was fast moving with short speeches," said one woman, a housewife from Walkerton, Ontario.

Her sister-in-law agreed. "I admired the honesty in those speeches. We have to get down and humble ourselves. You know, pride is the greatest sin of all. We are searching for the face of God rather than just sitting back and letting Him do things on His schedule."

Why did Canadians participate in a day of prayer on behalf of the American government?

"Well, communism may spread to North America," observed Cathy, a nurse in Toronto. "Christianity went West while communism went East. But now they've [the Communists] gone into Asia, Africa, Europe, South America and even the Caribbean. The Bible says that the Lord will protect Israel from Russia; but how strong are *we* in North America?"

Doug Burke, of Huntley Street, said, "At first, as it was primarily an American event, we were not going to go. But requests from our viewers flooded in. They asked if we could arrange a trip to Washington to pray with Americans. So we did."

"I think a similar thing has to happen in Canada," said the Walkerton housewife. "Every nation acknowledges God has been blessed by Him. What happens in the U.S. is an example to us."

When I asked Pastor Gimenez at the press conference if Washington for Jesus was planning to export the "Day of Prayer" to Canada, he answered, "When God calls, we go. We don't know about Canada yet. Now we are planning ones for New Zealand and Germany."

Later that night I got a chance to meet a born again who couldn't afford to be seen at the rally. Joe Barber was head of computer systems at a suburban Washington branch of IBM. He was a brash, opinionated fellow who had been born again just two years before. "People in my office would grab me by the short and curlies if they ever knew I came to this kind of thing. Who says there's freedom of religion in this country?" he demanded noisily as the bartender in the motel bar poured us each a drink. "You know what they are where I work? They are secular humanists," he snorted. "They are nearly Communists."

I laughed uneasily.

"Why are you laughing?" he demanded. "One day you...If you were in my shoes, you'd see it's no laughing matter."

I changed the subject and asked him why he wanted to meet me. "Well, Tim's an old friend of mine and he told me you were a Jew and along on the trip. I figured if I could convert you, I could carve another notch in my Bible—drink up."

Joe grew up in a rough neighbourhood in Brooklyn. He was born a Catholic, but as he became more and more successful in the business world, religion meant less and less to him. He still craved the "good life" he told me—wine, women and fun—but he was "on track" with Jesus. And there was no turning back this time.

He told me he had read the newspaper accounts of the rally and he didn't believe only 175,000 had attended. "It's because of those damn niggers," he said. "You know they pulled out at the last minute because their leaders figured that with all the southerners here it was bound to be a racist type of rally. Racism there. Balls! Balls! I say," he pounded the bar. The bartender looked up, amused.

Joe continued. "It's 'cause they're chickens, those Blacks, the lot of them. And if you weren't such a chicken you'd side with Jesus as well." When he saw his attempts to carve that notch in his Bible were wasted, he threw the money on the bar. "Well, Judy, nice meeting you. But I know some *real* Jews—and they'll talk turkey."

He lurched out into the night.

The ride back to Toronto was long and tortured. My last "interview" with Joe was pretty rough. I got a rather disturbing picture of the born-again community. Eighteen hours rolling around like peas in a tin can stretched before me.

I started to make the rounds. Bob Jackson is an ambulance driver in Bobcaygeon, Ontario. Technically he's retired, but since no one else will do it he still drives the ambulance, calls the fire department and sometimes rescues cats from trees. He is a member of the Full Gospel Businessmen's Fellowship and spends his spare time travelling to conventions and revival meetings. "I just know one day I'll meet you in Heaven, Judy. I know God loves you and I do know that much." I thanked him and moved on.

Tim introduced me to a couple with a small baby and to a woman friend who had come with him. They were members of a prayer fellowship centred at the couple's house in Mississauga, a suburb of Toronto. Mark, the husband, was the leader. "I guess you could say I am the 'spiritual leader' of the fellowship. But really we're all equal before the Lord."

His wife nodded sympathetically.

We chatted during the long ride home and got to know one another. Susie, the friend, was married but her husband couldn't get time off work so she came herself. She told me

she was one-quarter Jewish, but since she'd found God she
had never looked back.

"I'd love to see Americans at a Washington for Jesus in
Ottawa. I think Canadians could learn a lot in generosity and
hospitality from the U.S.," Susie said. "It's significant for any
country to make a stand and to repent before the world.
That's what Canada needs too."

As we piled off the bus in Toronto, I felt as if I had known
my new friends for a lot longer than three days. Susie felt it
too. She extended an invitation to their fellowship meetings
any Sunday morning.

"I don't want to carve a notch in *my* Bible," she smiled. "I
just want to give one of God's Chosen People another
chance."

# 2

# God Bless America

Getting to meet Jerry Falwell was not easy. At least not since two American freelancers sold an interview with him to *Penthouse* magazine. All interviews had to be pre-screened by his public relations director, Bill Faulkner. Faulkner and I arranged to meet at the stylish Hyatt Hotel, a stone's throw from the Capitol in downtown Washington, one short week after Ronald Reagan's election victory in November 1980.

I asked Faulkner how I would recognize him in the dining room—he told me not to worry because he would recognize me.

I arrived at the hotel early. At 7:30 a.m. three men in morning suits arrived and set up their music stands on a small stage surrounded by fall flowers. The Hyatt featured a classical chamber ensemble every weekday morning so that businessmen, lobbyists and politicians could crunch their cornflakes to Brahms and Mozart. The dining room seemed to be filled with clones of John Dean, scrubbed men in their 30s wearing horn rimmed glasses, dark blue suits and school ties partially hidden behind their *Wall Street Journal*s and their *Washington Post*s. Out of the corner of my eye I spotted a huge man in a vanilla suit, a dark shirt and a silver bola tie. He took off his Stetson when he shook my hand. His rings—signet, school and wedding—all dug into my palm. "I'm Bill Faulkner—and you must be the girl reporter," he smiled.

"How did you ever know me?"

"Well, I figured a pretty girl with glasses sitting alone and writing in a notebook was a good clue," he bellowed. Dozens of pairs of eyes left their newspapers. Dozens of eyebrows arched. It must have been some time since a reincarnation of Burl Ives playing Big Daddy interrupted their morning ritual.

Faulkner asked me all kinds of questions. Most I thought irrelevant to my desire to interview his boss. He explained how pleased he was to see that I was wearing a skirt. 'We often have to tell young reporters these days how to dress when they go see Dr. Falwell."

Finally he got around to asking if I were a Christian.

"No, I'm a Jew."

"Well!" he broke into a broad smile, patting my hand, "you are one of God's Chosen People, did you know that? Dr. Falwell just loves the ground the Jews walk on."

Several newspapers rustled.

The first rule was that I was to call Falwell "doctor." Why doctor?

"Well, he's got an honourary doctorate from Temple University; we like people to show a little respect."

"Do you mean Temple University near Philadelphia?" I enquired.

"Hell no," laughed Faulkner. "I mean Tennessee Temple Bible College in Nashville."

Doctor Falwell it would have to be.

Faulkner's final question was what was Canada like and had I ever watched The Old Time Gospel Hour up there? Yes, I had, I admitted.

"You know," mused Faulkner, "I've never been to Canada. Hell, I don't hardly know where Canada is. All I know is we get a lot of donations from there."

I had passed my interview with flying colours. "But where will I catch up with Dr. Falwell?" I asked Faulkner. He urged me to go to the I Love America rally several days hence in Trenton, New Jersey.

"But I've already run through three states chasing you

down; I can't run to Trenton as well."

But Faulkner was adamant. Falwell's schedule was tight and he'd have two hours for me just after the rally. Besides, the rally might be something I'd want to cover. Normally, Faulkner said, he'd only allow 15 minutes but since I had come such a long way, and I was so persistent, I could have as much time as I needed.

No one doubted the sincerity of the 2000 people who showed up for Jerry Falwell's I Love America rally in Trenton. You had to love America something powerful to overlook the bleak, grey downtown squalor that is the capital of New Jersey. I bundled up against the chill winds whistling down its almost deserted streets.

It is the 33rd I Love America rally at a state capital in 12 months presided over by the tough-talking evangelist from Lynchburg, Virginia and his clean-cut entourage.

Flanked by red, white and blue streamers and American flags, the man in the banker's blue three-piece suit rose to preach. As usual, Falwell minced no words.

"It is time that we join our efforts to turn this nation back to God. We do not like the moral drift of our nation. The landslide victory for conservative politics in the election gives us the energy to press on. We cannot allow vulgar, profane humanists to control history."

On cue, two dozen fresh-faced Liberty Baptist College Singers—from Falwell's own Liberty Baptist College—burst into "I Love America." They stepped neatly in time up and down the steps of the state capital building, singing, "Free to worship as we please...that's why I love America." Each singer flung one arm out to the side: "America, America." The other arm stretched up, and both reached out for the grand finale, "The land that I love. AMERICAAA."

"Everyone join hands," Falwell exhorted with a smile. "Homosexuals join hands too." He paused. "Oh, you have

Jerry Falwell

### Faith Partner Prayer Request

Please pray for me to be healed of
a broken hip, + for my husband to be given
what he needs to do the work, here,

### Faith Partner Prayer Request

Dear Jerry I have been feeling very bad + would
appreciate prayer

### Faith Partner Prayer Request

Healing for our son, Fred, who received
serious burns, in a furnace explosion
October 2. Psychological and physical
healing is needed
Thank you for interceding for us
Jesus bless your work!

# Congressional
# "REPORT CARD"

## HOW REPRESENTATIVE JOHN BRADEMAS VOTED ON 8 KEY MORAL ISSUES

### 96th CONGRESS - 1st SESSION
### JANUARY - DECEMBER, 1979

PREPARED ESPECIALLY FOR CHRISTIANS
by

CHRISTIAN
VOICE

MORAL GOVERNMENT FUND

Washington Office
418 "C" Street N.E.
Carriage House
Washington, D.C. 20002

Administrative Office
Post Office Box CFR
Pacific Grove, CA 93950

"When the righteous are in authority, the people rejoice: but when the wicked beareth rule, the people mourn." Prov. 29:2

---

Congressional "Report Card" issued by the right-wing Christian political action committee, The Christian Voice. (Continued on following pages.)

# HERE IS HOW YOUR REPRESENTATIVE, HON. JOHN BRADEMAS VOTED ON 8 KEY MORAL ISSUES DURING 1979

★★★★★★★★★★★★★★★★★★★★★★★★★★

| ISSUE | BRADEMAS VOTED | GRADE |
|---|---|---|
| 1. **CUTBACKS ON HUMANIST RESEARCH** <br> Ashbrook amendment to cut $4 million waste dollars from "behavioral research" (pro-humansit), including $88.830 for researching "homosexual couple formation" <br> HR 2729 | NO | Fail |
| 2. **FOR PRAYER IN SCHOOLS** <br> Walker amendment to require that daily opportunities for voluntary prayer be returned to children in classrooms. <br> HR 2444 | NO | Fail |
| 3. **FOR CHRISTIAN SCHOOLS** <br> Ashbrook amendment to stop the IRS from its repeated attempts to force the closing of private Christian schools by denying them tax exempt status. <br> HR 4393 | NO | Fail |
| 4. **FOR ABORTION** <br> Wilson substitute amendment to allow federal and locally raised revenues to be used in abortion funding. <br> Sub. Amend. | YES | Fail |
| 5. **AGAINST BUSING** <br> Mottl amendment to prohibit busing of children to schools outside their own neighborhoods. <br> HJ Res. 74 | NO | Fail |
| 6. **FOR BALANCED BUDGET** <br> Rousselot amendment to balance the budget and reduce inflation, thereby returning principles of financial stewardship to our government. <br> H. Con. Res. 186 | NO | Fail |
| 7. **ABORTION** <br> Wright motion to further increase abortion funding. <br> HR 4389 | YES | Fail |
| 8. **FOR PARENTAL CONSENT** <br> Dannemeyer motion to prevent children from being taught use of birth control devices in sex education classes without parental consent. <br> HR 4862 | NO | Fail |

From a fundamental Christian point of view, John Brademas failed as he voted on the above moral issues. Is he truly representing YOU in Washington? IF NOT, VOTE FOR CHANGE!

# NO,

YOUR MAN IN CONGRESS
**JOHN BRADEMAS**

we do not believe that America's Christians will remain silent while the country continues its slide towards national suicide! We DO believe that the rate of decline can be slowed down, and even reversed, if the "sleeping giant of American politics" (as the Congressional Quarterly referred to the Christian community) will rouse itself to become informed and involved.

AMERICA WAS FOUNDED BY MEN OF FAITH ON GODLY PRINCIPLES! That foundation has been our strength in the past. But the decline we have witnessed in recent years - morally, fiscally, and as a respected world leader - is directly traceable to the fact that fewer men in government truly adhere to those principles, and often fail to reflect them in their decisions.

A RETURN TO MORAL ACCOUNTABILITY on the part of these men is imperative if we, as a nation, are to survive. Jesus said, " ... occupy til I come!" He also said, "You are the salt (preservative) of the earth; if the salt has lost its savor (is no longer acting as a preservative), wherewith shall it be salted (what will act as a preservative)?" We cannot, in other words, rely on ungodly men and women to preserve this nation!

WE MUST BECOME INFORMED ABOUT THE MEN WHO REPRESENT US: and the laws which they pass or reject. Because, in the final analysis, it is we and our children who must live by those laws.

To that end, the CHRISTIAN VOICE MORAL GOVERNMENT FUND is providing you with a record of how YOUR elected representative voted on key moral issues during 1979. This information is taken directly from official government voting records on file in Washington, D.C. Remember as you study this voting record that if your representative does not represent your views in the United States Congress, ONLY YOU, as a voting member of his district, can vote for a change!

JOHN BRADEMAS DESERVES YOUR PRAYERS - BUT NOT YOUR VOTES REGISTER TO VOTE IN 1980 - OUR LIVES DEPEND ON IT!

already."

The crowd pealed with laughter at a small counter-demonstration on the fringe of the rally. A few polite protesters were carrying signs. "Gay Rights Mean Human Rights," "Support the ERA," and "Jerry's Mansion is on Earth."

In a brief ten years, the tables had been turned. Richard Nixon's "silent majority" had found its voice and given itself a promotion to "Moral Majority." And, as its chief spokesman, Jerry Falwell, more than any of the dozen or so nationally known television preachers, symbolized and lead the religious "New Right" in the U.S. More than any of the others, he had thrown himself and his forces headlong into the political fray.

Falwell, who has claimed his TV show, The Old Time Gospel Hour, is watched by 25 million people every Sunday, heads a religious empire with annual contributions in excess of $50 million. Like most of the TV evangelists, Falwell actively shunned politics until just before the 1980 presidential election. But, in January 1979, he founded the Moral Majority, a right-wing political lobby group, and it quickly shot to prominence in the homestretch of the 1980 presidential campaign. The Moral Majority claimed to have activated ten million people, registered four million "Christian" voters, recruited two million members, and took modest credit not only for the Reagan victory, but also for the fact that liberal senators and congressmen on its hit list, such as George McGovern, Frank Church, and Birch Bayh, went down like dominoes.

Some, like John Buchanan, a Republican congressman from Alabama for 16 years, were wiped out as far back as the primaries by candidates supported by the Moral Majority—in Buchanan's case by a former member of the Ku Klux Klan. Buchanan's case was special. He is a devout Baptist minister and a self-professed born-again Christian. But like another born-again politician, Jimmy Carter, his piety helped him not a whit when the zealots zeroed in on his politics and pronounced them un-Christian. He was denounced as an opponent of prayer in the schools and as soft on abortion and welfare rights. Volunteers bombarded churches throughout his district with pamphlets. One such leaflet from Jerry Jenkins, a Moral Majority activist from Woodlawn Church of Christ in Birmingham, read in part: "I am trying to let our membership in the Birmingham area know of the liberal voting record of John Buchanan. I believe his record is against the principles of righteousness.

"Because moral issues are involved, I believe that Christians have the privilege, and even the obligation, to take a stand for the Lord...I do not believe the church needs to be involved in political matters, but because the incumbent representative has voted so frequently against what is right, I am making this request."

When I interviewed him in his Washington office, John Buchanan, a tall, grey-haired imposing figure, exuded Southern charm and looked the very model of a U.S. congressman. Among the mementoes of his years in office, his staff hung a banner over the doorway: "Home of the Immoral Minority." Says Buchanan of his defeat, "I'd say they did a rather thorough job of beating my brains out with Christian love."

Shortly after the 1980 election, Falwell issued a general warning to Republicans and Democrats alike. "Get in step," he cautioned, or "be prepared to be unemployed."

Far from content with the new Congress, the Moral Majority intended to see its ideals become reality. Among these were returning the U.S. to military and political pre-eminence, outlawing abortion, putting prayer back in the schools and curbing the rights of homosexuals.

Pornography was another target for the crusaders. Ironically, Falwell at that time was locked in legal combat with *Penthouse* magazine. The March 1981 issue carried a

5000 word interview with him. Claiming that he had no idea
the interview would appear in the "salacious, vulgar
magazine," Falwell won a temporary injunction to stop
distribution of the issue. Later, he dropped it.

His "Clean Up America Campaign" (yes, it's a genuine
Falwell trademark) doesn't stop there. From the pulpit of his
Thomas Road Baptist Church, Falwell called for a return to
the "McCarthy era, where we register all Communists. We
should stamp it on their foreheads and send them back to
Russia."

Falwell's view of America's role in international affairs
has been: "speak softly but carry a big stick." He has, for
example, lobbied for strong U.S. support for the state of
Israel. "The Jews are the Chosen People of God. I'm walking
around blessing them wherever I go."

At best this is a mixed blessing. At the Richmond, Virginia
I Love America rally, Falwell said to his audience, "I know
why you don't like the Jew; he can make more money
accidentally than you can make on purpose."

"Yes, I said that, but I said it jokingly," Falwell told me.
"Someone felt I was stereotyping Jews by making that
comment. I don't have any problem with it. It was purely a
joke." But leaders of the American Jewish community were
not laughing, especially in light of remarks by other
evangelists such as Falwell's cohort, Bailey Smith, president
of the Southern Baptist Convention, who announced that
"Almighty God does not hear the prayer of the Jews." Jewish
leaders have feared the effects of these "jokes," for the line
between a joke and a racial slur is often too fine for even an
angel to dance upon.

In an October 1981 broadcast of The Old Time Gospel
Hour, Falwell candidly admitted that his support of Israel
and the Jews brought him "more hate letters and death
threats than any other issue with which I have been
involved." Like sorcerer's apprentices, Falwell and other
evangelical leaders have expressed naive astonishment at the
awesome reservoir of bigotry lurking in their constituency

and at the powerful forces of reaction they are capable of inciting.

Jeffrey Hadden and Charles Swann in their book *Prime Time Preachers: The Rising Power of Televangelism* comment, perhaps somewhat charitably to Falwell and others of the New Christian Right:

> At the edge of the left and the right stand spokesmen for a lunatic fringe who do hear voices or are otherwise confident that they have both special insights about what is wrong with society and a mandate to pursue their goals. The United States is currently experiencing a resurgence of Ku Klux Klan and anti-Semitic activities the like of which we have not experienced for many years. So also are we experiencing a new boldness by religious bigots. . . .
>
> The leaders of the New Christian Right would like to believe that such happenings are unrelated to their social movement. . . . The lunatic fringe may not be the constituency of the New Christian Right, but the latter's success certainly gives those who commit excesses reason to believe that their acts are acceptable and legitimate. . . .
>
> The credibility of the New Christian Right may well be defined in terms of how it reacts to those who stand on the same end of the political spectrum but beyond the consensual rules of U.S. politics. Given the semi-autonomous nature of Moral Majority chapters, this may well be Jerry Falwell's greatest challenge.

Rabbi Alexander Schindler, president of the Union of American Hebrew Congregations, warned a San Francisco meeting of Jewish leaders that it was "no coincidence that the rise of right-wing Christian fundamentalism has been accompanied by the most serious outbreak of anti-Semitism in America since World War II."

Nevertheless, in November 1980, then-Israeli Prime

Minister Menachem Begin, on a fundraising drive through the U.S., awarded Jerry Falwell the Jabotinsky Centennial Medal for his "service to Israel." Some members of the Jewish community were skeptical. Begin and other leaders of the Israeli government have often used expediency to justify unsavoury alliances. The late Senator Frank Church of Idaho, himself a strong supporter of Israel, flatly refused the same medal because Falwell was a recipient.

Rabbi Schindler also cautioned against assuming that support for Israel among evangelists is rooted in respect for the Jews. "They believe Jesus cannot return for the second coming until the Jews are grouped in their biblical homeland and then converted to Christianity...They believe further that even devout Jews are not welcome in heaven." It should be noted that Schindler is by no means Falwell's strongest critic.

In the more general political arena, Falwell's crusade has polarized Americans in one of the fiercest debates in recent U.S. history. The counter-attack against Falwell and the Moral Majority, however, got under way too late to make any difference in the 1980 election. The American Civil Liberties Union (ACLU) bought a number of full-page ads in the *New York Times* at a cost of $20,000 each right after the election. The headline read: "If the Moral Majority has its way, you'd better start praying." Ira Glasser, executive director of the ACLU, said of the Moral Majority, "They have helped to block passage of the ERA in 15 states; they want prayer put back in the schools; they want to make abortion illegal. They are trying to take the Bill of Rights away from Americans." The ACLU ad called for Americans to join the campaign to fight the new anti-Bill of Rights movement.

Jack Anderson, a syndicated Washington columnist and number-one muckraking journalist in the U.S., went to perhaps the heart of the matter. "A fundamentalist Christian crusade called the Moral Majority endorsed one congressman who was caught soliciting sex and another who was

photographed accepting a bribe [in the Abscam case].
Apparently, the Moral Majority admired them more for their
conservative politics than their Christian morality."

It has been noted that Falwell rarely talks about age-old
Christian values such as duty, obligation to the poor or the
spirit of brotherhood. "There are more than 3000 verses in
the Bible on the commitment to the poor, to justice and
righteousness, but they are silent on that," remarked Rev.
Tom Skinner, a born-again Black activist and critic of the
Moral Majority.

Congressman Paul Simon of Illinois, himself a victim of
the evangelical right's rating game, agreed. "The nearest
scriptural base for a 'rating' that I can recall is in Matthew 25,
the judgment day scene, where Christ lists the questions we
will be asked: Did you help the hungry? Did you give water
to the thirsty? Did you provide clothes to those needing
them? Did you take care of the sick? Did you show concern
for those in prison?" Simon explained that Falwell and his ilk
are reluctant to address these questions. "Somehow they
improved on that almost 2000-year-old list so none of the
original concerns are reflected. But I have little sympathy for
those who equate their position with God's position, who in
a simplistic and non-scriptural way confuse theology and
politics."

Patricia Roberts Harris, a Black woman and former U.S.
Secretary of Health and Human Services in the Carter
Administration, lashed out at the religious right: "The
absolute certainty with which some individuals approach the
political battle and the arrogance with which they propose a
crusade to 're-Christianise America' is dangerous for our
democracy."

But the most spectacular attack came in a series of slick,
professional prime-time TV ads by satirist Norman Lear,
originator of TV shows All in the Family and Mary Hartman,
Mary Hartman. "People for the American Way" is the
organization Lear founded specifically to take on the Moral
Majority. In a fundraising letter he wrote: "If I live to be a

# Dr. Jerry Falwell

εThe Richmond New Leader
333 E. Grace St
Religion Editor
Richmond, Virginia  23219

Dear Friend:

I cannot carry this burden much longer.  I am being torn in all directions.

And that's why I left my office and came home early today to write you this letter.

For the first time in my 23 years of preaching Christ on the Old-Time Gospel Hour television and radio network, I'm prayerfully considering taking the program off the air.

I must confess to you that right now I am not absolutely sure that the Old-Time Gospel Hour is the most effective tool we can use during the 1980's to save our nation.

Because of financial pressures on me caused by inflation and recession -- we are simply not ready for the decade ahead of us.  And this "Decade of Destiny" for America is less than 90 days away.

I believe that God has called me to be an instrument in His hand to bring this nation back to God.

And I have always felt that God raised up the Old-Time Gospel Hour as His way of helping me accomplish the vision He has given me.

But unless the Old-Time Gospel Hour is financially prepared for the challenge of the decade of the 80's -- then I must ask God to show me another way to help bring spiritual awakening to Richmond, Virginia -- and our nation.

εThe Richmond New Leader, I was thrilled  when the Lord led you to join the Old-Time Gospel Hour family of friends.

---

Personalized fundraising letter to a daily newspaper which found its way onto Falwell's list of Faith Partners.

I am praying -- with deep conviction -- that you will be able to send a gift of $15...

...and check "YES" on your commitment card to fast and pray ... that God will save America.

If you answer "YES", I will send you a copy of a book I have recently written entitled, 'Fasting and Prayer' -- the Hope for America.

£The Richmond New Leader, please believe me, with God as my judge, I am dead serious about shutting down the Old-Time Gospel Hour.

If this ministry is not ordained by God to bring America to revival in the next decade, I don't want it to continue.

I must know what God wants. The fleece is out, the financial pressure must be removed.

That's why your special gift of $15 means so much to me.

If we are not ready to be God's instrument -- we must go off the air. And God must then show me how He wants us to reach and save this nation.

I have prayed that God will send me a sign -- yes or no -- and that sign will be an Army of One Million people who will fast and pray with me on October 14th.

Your Friend in Christ,

Jerry Falwell

P.S.   One last prayerful word, my friend ...

...if there is any way possible you can send an even larger gift than $15 right now -- please do so. Maybe you can even double that amount.

And remember to send back your Prayer and Fasting Commitment Card to me immediately.

Please let me know right away that you are standing by me.

This is the only way I will know if God wants me to keep the Old-Time Gospel Hour on the air.

thousand—I may never write a letter more important than this one. The future of our pluralistic society is at stake. . . . You have been witnessing, I am sure, the growth of the religious-oriented New Right. . . . The danger of the Religious New Right is not that they are speaking out on political issues, which is their right, if not their obligation; it is the way they attack the integrity and character of anyone who does not stand with them."

In one TV ad, a worker in a lumberjack shirt points to his wife and son. The man explains that he is a Protestant, his wife a Catholic, and his son is somewhere in between. But the family, despite its diverse religious beliefs, is God-fearing and American. Another TV commercial shows a southern woman vacuuming her living room. She stops and faces the camera. She says that she is a born-again Christian and loves the life south of the Mason-Dixon line, but she still feels that everyone is entitled to his own political views and should not be dictated to by religious leaders. "That's the American Way, isn't it?" she challenges the viewers.

But despite themselves, the Lear ads stooped to the level of the Moral Majority. Running through the television pieces was a powerful appeal to that lowest common denominator of American life—national chauvinism. And rather than discounting the idea that one must be a good Christian to be a good American, the ads reinforced the supreme virtues of God and country.

If nothing else, the evangelical right have made their enemies fight them on their own ground in a spitting contest over who is more patriotic and God-fearing.

But it was strictly no contest. After all, Jerry Falwell, a former highschool football star who once turned down an offer to play baseball with the St. Louis Cardinals, has claimed to converse with God "daily." He says without a flicker of doubt, "The entire Bible, from Genesis to Revelation, is the inerrant word of God and totally accurate in all respects."

Well over six feet tall, Falwell dresses in somber three-piece suits and matching ties. He sports a bronze "Jesus First" lapel button ("You get two absolutely free when you write or call the Old Time Gospel Hour") and a stickpin of Old Glory. He can't escape his television persona. Even in a personal interview his gaze is slightly uplifted and beyond the interviewer, as if he's making every point a pitch to a TV audience. Falwell radiates absolute authority. His tone is intended to put the fear of God into his listeners although he is more careful about his pronouncements in person than he is in the pulpit. He tends to raise his voice whenever he discusses politics or his favourite target, "secular humanists."

Falwell is the quintessential big brother. On the road, for instance at the I Love America rally, he totes an entourage which would put many a presidential candidate to shame. In addition to half a dozen security men who also wear three-piece suits, he has two dozen Liberty Baptist Singers, a public relations man, Faulkner, an appointment secretary, and his wife, Macel. Falwell also brings along two or three cousins from "down home Virginia way" who lend a common touch. Falwell's cousins were given an ovation at a pastor's luncheon I attended after the rally in Trenton. The cousins don't have much to say, but their presence kindles feelings of warmth, family and trust, especially among the unconverted. Wherever he travels, press people jostle and push to get close enough for a few words.

Brother Falwell, as he is called by other born-again pastors, draws the line at smoking, drinking and dancing. Most movies and TV shows, like Three's Company and Charlie's Angels, are out. Walt Disney movies are in.

Wes Beals, a student at Falwell's Liberty Baptist College, explained that a typical date included "bowling or watching a Walt Disney movie. It's exciting. We have a good time."

Students at the college must double-date until their final year, when single dates are permitted. There is no inter-racial dating allowed unless it is okayed by the parents. Many students have replaced their car radios with tape decks and

cassettes of religious music, like the college's own Liberty
Baptist Singers or the Bells of Liberty.

Falwell likes to see women wear skirts and men wear
pants: after all, he had just thundered at the Trenton rally,
"God created Adam and Eve, not Adam and Steve!"

I met with Falwell right after the rally. He was in good
spirits. Sipping a can of Coke in a shabby downtown
Trenton hotel room, he relaxed.

"You know, you're the first Canadian to interview me," he
drawled. "You Canadians are so polite. One more thing I just
want to mention, thank you for rescuing our embassy boys
from Iran." He beamed.

I asked him if he had any plans to expand his ministry into
Canada. "Not at this time," he told me. "We're not really
involved up there at all. As a U.S. citizen I feel that the
government of Canada extends a privilege for us to operate
in Canada at all. As an American, I know what we have to
do to turn this country around. But I'm not a Canadian and
don't want to meddle in affairs that aren't mine. [However, a
couple of years later, Falwell caused a minor stir in U.S.-
Canada relations when he labelled then-Prime Minister
Trudeau a "Leninist."] Occasionally I speak up in Canada
and my show is on many TV stations there—we've got a
good response from Canadians."

How much money does he get from Canada? Without
hesitating he replied, "Well, the Old Time Gospel Hour made
$60 million last year in the U.S. I don't know what it made in
Canada. I do know that all the money stays in Canada and is
spent on buying TV air time and so on. Not a penny goes for
politics. There's no mixing of funds from the Moral Majority
to the Old Time Gospel Hour."

Falwell is a very recent convert to political activism; for
years he had been a leader in preaching against the church's
involvement in politics. On March 21, 1965, the same day
that hundreds of clergymen joined with civil rights workers
for a march on Montgomery, Alabama, Falwell delivered a
sermon chastising the clergy for their involvement in civil

rights.

"I would find it impossible to stop preaching the pure saving gospel of Jesus Christ, and begin doing anything else—including fighting communism, or participating in civil rights
reforms. . . . Preachers are not called to be politicians but to
be soul winners. . . . The gospel does not clean up the outside
but rather regenerates the inside."

How could Falwell and many other evangelicals have
changed their minds so radically? Falwell simply says he was
wrong before and he's right now, and that's that. But it
doesn't hurt that the issues have become more to his liking.

"A lot of anti-family measures that the previous
government has taken has forced us into the political arena,"
he explained to me. "In 1973, the Roe versus Wade decision
by the Supreme Court legalized abortion on demand; now
there is a $54 billion pornography business in the U.S.; gay
rights and the attempt to stifle students and staff in the
Christian schools is another thing. Either we waive the right
to be involved or we address the political questions."

With Reagan elected and liberal congressmen and senators
defeated, what is the need for the Moral Majority?

"We started the Moral Majority to deal with moral
principles. We are strongly pro-life, pro-family, pro-morality
and pro-defence. We happened to get caught up in an
election. Our work is cut out for us. We have to work now to
get the Human Life Amendment passed, the Voluntary
Prayer in the Schools Amendment passed and the Family
Protection Act passed. If the leaders of Christendom in the
nation don't stand up against immorality, we can't expect
anyone to lead. I think it's the duty of gospel preachers to set
the pace."

Falwell sees his ministry in the vanguard of a "holy war
against moral cancers."

"The local church is an organized army equipped for
battle, ready to charge the enemy," he emphasized. "The
church should be a disciplined, charging army. . . . Christians,
like slaves and soldiers, ask no questions."

In his booklet, *The Future, the Bible and You,* Falwell shows why the United States is especially important to God. "America has the largest percentage of born-again believers of any nation on earth. Jesus said to Christians, 'Ye are the salt of the earth.' Salt is a preservative. Because of the Christians in America, God has a hedge around this nation. The infidels and those who hate God and the church are enjoying the highest standard of living the world has ever known because they live around much salt.

"...America will remain important to God only as she commits herself to evangelizing and winning to Christ her own inhabitants...."

Lynchburg is a town of 100,000 in the Piedmont area of Virginia. It has quiet tree-lined streets, frame houses and children who call you "Ma'am" when you ask directions. It used to be a segregated southern town until segregation was outlawed, but there is still a White side and a Black side of town. Lynchburg is also the base of operations for the huge Falwell empire and Jerry's home town.

All the townspeople know "Dr. Falwell's church," the Thomas Road Baptist Church, and are quick to point it out to visitors. One elderly woman told me, "I don't like the church and what it stands for but you just have to get used to the idea that Falwell runs this town." Rumour has it that a short time ago, his ministry tried to buy all the drinking establishments in town when their leases came up in an effort to clean up Lynchburg.

A variety of slick pamphlets produced by his church explain his conversion to Christianity. Though his father was an alcoholic who had no use for religion, Falwell's mother tuned into radio evangelist Charles Fuller's Old Fashioned Revival Hour every Sunday morning. Falwell, who claims he was "too lazy to get out of bed and turn off the radio," listened to the show for years. After two years of engineering at the secular Lynchburg College and two days in training camp "Jerry rejected the call of the St. Louis Cardinals and accepted the call of God."

He quit Lynchburg College and enrolled at Baptist Bible College in Springfield, Missouri. After graduation, he started his own ministry back in Lynchburg in a building abandoned by the Donald Duck Bottling Company. In the intervening 30 years, the original congregation of 35 people has grown to 17,000—the largest in the U.S. His operating budget in 1979 was $56 million and his empire includes the Thomas Road Baptist Church, private elementary and high schools, and Liberty Baptist College and Seminary just outside town on his own Liberty Mountain. "They used to call us the Donald Duck Baptist Church," Falwell laughs. "Now we reach more people than Lawrence Welk."

The Old Time Gospel Hour is produced live every Sunday from the main sanctuary of the church. Business is always brisk. Outside the auditorium in the lobby is a booth which sells records by the Liberty Baptist Singers and the Bells of Liberty, the two choirs which make up the travelling sideshow that accompanies Falwell on his trips.

Another kiosk displays information packages for the press and offers a basket of free lapel pins, some of the American flag, and some that twinkle "Jesus First."

The attractive middle-aged woman behind the counter beckoned me. She reached underneath and pulled out a small basket of stick pins with a red maple leaf. "These what you're looking for?" she smiled. "They might be made in the U.S. of A. but they are the Canadian flag. Y'all come back now, y'hear?"

The church was filled to capacity. In a sea of 5000 faces, a scattering of blacks stood out. The audience was all ages. The huge number of young people took me by surprise. "People come from all over the U.S. just to attend a service," one of the ushers told me.

Falwell figures between 25 and 50 million watch his show. The truth is, closer to a half-million people watch the show each week. How did Falwell get his figures? By proclamation, say authors Jeffrey Hadden and Charles Swann. "Jerry Falwell uses the phrase 'ministerially speaking' to joke about his exaggerations of his audience size and other numbers," Hadden and Swann write. "It's as if the preacher's cloak gives him license to embellish in the name of the Lord. . . . Bigger is better even in religion."

But the Old Time Gospel Hour is only the sixth top-rated religious show on television, behind those of Oral Roberts, Rex Humbard and Robert Schuller's Hour of Power. Even so, his one-hour telecast is transmitted to over 373 stations in the U.S. and his 30-minute daily radio programme is heard on 300 stations.

How does he do it?

The one-hour televised service is spiked with no less than ten fundraising pitches—from personal requests from Falwell, to asking viewers to mail $5 for a paperback book written by a guest who gave a sermon. The litany of appeals is never-ending.

For $10 a month, a viewer can become a Faith Partner and receive Falwell's monthly newsletter, a special edition of the King James Bible and two bronze and one gold-plated Jesus First lapel pins.

The day I attended, Falwell asked for any one-time givers to declare themselves "Prayer Warriors," that is, to send in their names and indicate which five-minute period in the day they will set aside to pray for the ministry. For $12 a month, the viewer can also join the I Love America Club, which issues a monthly "Clean Up America Hotline Report" and lets members know where and when Falwell will be preaching. In addition, members receive a special bicentennial Bible.

Any tax-deductible gift will enrol a person in the Liberty Missionary Society, which "channels millions of dollars to help mission outreaches worldwide. . . . Thousands of souls will be in glory because of the concern for the friends of the Liberty Missionary Society."

More than 10,000 students are enrolled in Falwell's Liberty

Home Bible Study course at a cost of $23 a month. An additional pledge will allow the student or TV viewer to become a friend of the Liberty Mountain Scholar Share programme, which ensures that "young champions for Christ may receive proper guidance and training that they may best serve the Lord."

Viewers are urged to remember the ministry in their wills, and there is a special number to call if you need assistance in "estate planning."

But the largest amount of income is not collected in such random appeals. They are only the beginning. Falwell's secret of success, and that of other "televangelists," lies in the use of huge computerized databanks which store, retrieve and sort personal information contained in the tens of thousands of pieces of mail the Old Time Gospel Hour receives every week. Here are some actual examples of Falwell's "Faith Partner Prayer Requests" that I had the opportunity to see.

Dear Sir: My prayer request is for my tongue. Since my stroke it has been bothering me because it won't stay in my mouth. Thank you very much. I'm sorry but this is all I can afford.

Dear Rev. Falwell: My pledge is $5 a month. I said I would give. I just cannot afford any more. Lord, if I could be healed of arthritis in my back and hands I've prayed day in and day out. Also someone to write my memoirs of 83 years. Thank you Lord and Dr. Falwell.

Pray that I will receive a blessing, a miracle. I need money to pay bills, medical bills over $5,000.00. That does not include my house payment, insurance, clothes and shoes for my two sons and my household bills. I am praying for a miracle. If you know where I can get help for finances, please let me know. I need help. Pray for me.

Remember me in your prayers. It sometimes gets rather lonesome without Alfred, he passed away Oct. 9, 1979, a little more than a year ago. He loved your programs, so do I. Will remember you in prayer and fasting for America Nov. 2.

Healing for our son, Fred, who received serious burns in a furnace explosion Oct. 2. Psychological and physical healing is needed. Thank you for interceding for us. Jesus bless your work.

The first request was presumably entered into the computer under "strokes," the second under "arthritis," the third under "financial" and so on. These are cross-filed with the people's pledges, age, how many times they've given and how much, and what future contributions can be expected from them.

Since all the authors of these letters are Faith Partners, each will receive a monthly personalized computer-written letter from Falwell. Enclosed with the letter will be a Prayer Request form bearing the contributor's name.

Similarly, the name will be computer-printed in the salutation on the first page of the letter and a couple of standard "hope the Lord has helped heal your arthritis" paragraphs will be slugged into the format. The following pages will be the same as thousands of others receive, with an appeal for funds in the closing paragraphs.

Somehow, the afternoon newspaper in Richmond, Virginia received a "personal" letter from Falwell that is much like a letter to an ailing Faith Partner. Falwell wrote:

I cannot carry this burden much longer. I am being torn in all directions. And that's why I left my office and came home early today to write you this letter. . . . Because of financial pressures on me caused by inflation and recession—we are simply not ready for the decade ahead of us. And this "Decade of Destiny" for America is less than 90 days away....But unless the Old Time Gospel Hour is financially prepared for the challenge of the decade of the '80s—then I must ask God to show me another way to help bring spiritual awakening to Richmond, Virginia—and our nation.

The Richmond News Leader, I was thrilled when the Lord led you to join the Old Time Gospel Hour family of friends.

...Write down your prayer requests on the bottom of your Prayer and Fasting Commitment Card and send it back to me immediately.

Because on Sunday, October 14th, we will pray for your needs, The Richmond News Leader....I assure you—your prayer will receive individual attention on Oct. 14th.

...I am praying—with deep conviction—that you will be able to send a gift of $15...The Richmond News Leader, please believe me, with God as my judge, I am dead serious about shutting down the Old Time Gospel Hour. That's why your special gift of $15 means so much to me.

Hadden and Swann explain: "The computer provides a sort of technological equivalent of the Book of Judgment. It lets the preacher divide the sheep from the goats, those who offer golden fleece from the stubborn goats who don't grow any or won't share any. Its practical value is that it allows the preachers to mount a giant direct-mail campaign, sending out millions of fund-raising letters as if passing one huge collection plate. And it allows the preachers to run economical direct-mail systems by concentrating on the names and addresses that pay off well enough to support their multi-million dollar programming costs."

Falwell contends that separation of church and state does not mean separation of God and government.

"We are a republic governed by laws predicated upon the Bible," writes Falwell in *The Future, the Bible, and You.* "God has elevated and promoted this nation to a greatness no other nation has ever enjoyed. . . .

"Revival is the only hope for America. We must become aware of sin. As we see those philosophical differences that are taking this nation away from where she originally started, we must pray, preach, teach and live as never before. . . . We need to have a grass-roots revival in order to bring America back to God; if we don't we are going to lose our liberties and our freedoms. While this responsibility lies with our decision makers, it must also be shared by all of us. We must let our leaders know how we feel regarding these basic moral right and wrong decisions."

Falwell has already marched farther along the road to political power than most evangelists in American history. Does Falwell intend to take the final plunge and go for political office? "No," he answered with a smile, "I can fight better from the outside."

# 3

# For He's a Jolly Good Felon

It was hard to believe the man across the table from me in his room in a suburban Toronto Holiday Inn was once the second-most powerful man in the United States. Charles W. Colson, former special counsel to U.S. President Richard Nixon and self-proclaimed "tough guy," was dubbed the "hatchet man" of the White House.

Chuck Colson, Watergate felon. He served time in prison and got out early for good behaviour. Who had not heard about the bugging of the Democratic Party headquarters; the subsequent investigation; the eventual resignation of Nixon and the imprisonment of his top aides?

In 1974, Colson was found guilty of conspiracy to burglarize the office of Daniel Ellsberg's psychiatrist. Tried and convicted, Colson spent seven months behind bars.

Just before his imprisonment, he became a born-again Christian. While in jail, he started prayer and Bible Study sessions with other inmates. Upon his release, he founded Prison Fellowship International, a Washington-based evangelical ministry that brings inmates who are "committed Christians" out of jail in the middle of their sentences, trains them to be "Christian leaders" and sends them back inside, not to "serve time" but to "serve Jesus with their time."

Colson calls these prisoners "God's secret agents," a phrase of special significance to a man who had risen to the apex of power during the early 70s and who was described in *All the President's Men* as one of the "original back-room-boys... the brokers, the guys who fix things when they break down and do the dirty work when it's necessary."

While others involved in the Watergate coverup renounced their pasts, wrote books and articles turning the dirt of the Nixon years into gold, only Colson and the infamous Gordon Liddy have been constant in their wholehearted support of Nixon, then and now. During the Watergate investigation, Colson told the *Washington Post*: "I will not discuss private communications between myself and the President—not with anyone, you, the press in general, with the Grand Jury or the Senate Committee."

It is not as if, however, Colson hasn't had his share of the gold. In 1976, Colson's autobiography, *Born Again*, became an overnight bestseller, selling almost half-a-million copies in hardcover alone. It was followed by a movie of the same title in 1978 starring Anne Francis and Dana Andrews. It is the story of his conversion to Christianity. In 1979, its sequel, *Life Sentence* (over 100,000 copies in hardcover), chronicled the years following Colson's incarceration, his work with prisoners and the start of Prison Fellowship International, which is now a "worldwide" evangelical organization. A Canadian ministry took shape shortly thereafter. Colson's promotional tabloid *Hope* claimed 4000 volunteers for Prison Fellowship and 40 staff members at its Washington headquarters. Among its long-range goals is to have a "Care Committee in each community surrounding every State or Federal prison," to "build relationships between people inside and outside prisons."

According to David Farrell, a lawyer with the Department of Justice in Ottawa who took a leave of absence to become its first executive director, the Prison Fellowship of Canada offered a unique service.

"We go into the prisons and 'care' for the men," he told me on the phone. "Then we turn them to Christ. We are gentle in our techniques and we don't use high-powered preaching to get our point across. To call us simply 'born again' is putting the wrong label on this ministry. We sponsor weekly fellowships with men in prison; and we are soon going to have seminars inside prisons, and the chance for inmates to go outside the walls for one-day seminars—just like Colson does in the States."

Prison Fellowship of Canada was formally launched at a founding dinner in Ottawa, October 8, 1980. Forty people from a variety of backgrounds attended, including labour leaders, MP's, prison and justice officials and ex-prisoners. The 12 board members include Shirley Carr, a vice-president of the Canadian Labour Congress, Leslie Tarr, editor of *Faith Today*, and as president and chairman, former Liberal cabinet minister Paul Hellyer. Also on the board are Charles "Chuck" Colson, who was the keynote speaker at the dinner, and Gordon Loux, also an American and executive vice-president of Colson's outfit.

Prison Fellowship has status as a charitable organization, and publishes a newsletter called *Canadian Jubilee*. It spent $97,000 in 1981 and $94,000 in 1982. This modest budget is supplemented by volunteer work and its early deficit was covered by fundraising in late 1980.


Sitting across from Colson, a couple of cans of Coke on a formica table between us (he doesn't drink alcohol), I got a close look at the man of Watergate fame. He wore the familiar horn-rimmed glasses and a pin-striped suit.

It had not been easy to get an interview with him. He had spoken at a *Faith Today* fundraising dinner I attended the previous evening, and autographed copies of *Life Sentence*. The next day, he was going to minister to prisoners at Collins Bay Penitentiary. As a man devoted to his cause, Colson hardly cares whether the press knows about him, likes him, or publicizes his sorties into jail. If I expected his born-again experience to produce a kindly man, I was wrong. He still plays hardball—for another team.

When I phoned his hotel room to make the appointment, I had to be screened by his personal bodyguard *cum* secretary, David Bovenizer. After I told him I was writing a story for the *Canadian Churchman*, the Anglican Church's national newspaper, he was quick to ask its circulation. Then he asked if I was born again and, if not, was I pro- or anti-evangelical?

Bovenizer was disappointed when I told him the circulation was 270,000. "Is that all?" he drawled.

"Yes—that's like 2.7 million in the U.S.," I replied.

"Well," he snorted, "I guess an interview couldn't hurt."

I understood better what Bovenizer meant by "hurt" when I knocked on the door of the second floor motel room. Bovenizer blocked the door, a bull of a man. He was tall, with horn-rimmed glassés and straight hair with a cowlick. Muscles rippled under his pale button-down shirt. His manicured hands were the size of baseball mitts. Just under the arm that was barricading the doorway, through the sliver of light, I spotted Colson at the coffee table near the window, Bible open.

Bovenizer introduced himself as Mr. Colson's appointment secretary and ushered me in.

Colson's height surprised me. He too was well over six feet; his bulkiness he attributes to his wife Patty's excellent cooking. The boyish face is set off by nearly comical, black, horn-rimmed glasses. His eyes are very blue but never twinkle.

"Well," he said clasping my hand, "It's good to meet another Christian."

I explained I was a Jew, there to write a story for an Anglican publication. For a minute he was stumped, but then he barked, "All right, give me the questions you have and let's get this interview over with."

Oh, that Watergate charm. Stretched out on one of the double beds, Bovenizer rumbled, "That's right, Chuck, we've got to go soon."

"Wait a minute," I protested, "You said I could have half

an hour."

Colson was irritated. "Let's just get started and see how far we can get."

Colson kicked off: "I used to think I'd been successful at everything I'd done, but only when I lost everything did I find *real* security. I was a Nixon law-and-order man; I wrote his speeches; every day 12 senior men and I assembled in the Roosevelt Room to decide the fate of the United States for that day. We got excited about tinkering up the old U.S. of A. government but as Tolstoy said, 'It's the passions—not the brains that change how people live.'"

Colson launched into his philosophy. "The real issue today is not socialism vs. capitalism; it is the age-old battle between good and evil. And that battle is being fought in the human heart. And the problems in the hearts of lots of people are their values. Why not fulfill your own ego and gratify yourself? Do your own thing," he roared. "It's invaded our culture; look at the moral decay of our society. Abortion is argued on a social level rather than a moral one. There is homosexuality. There is the break-up of the family. There are 1.1 million unmarried couples in the U.S., and the divorce rate is surpassing marriages. We'll run out of families in the U.S. before we run out of gas."

Colson's lofty criticism of American society was very much in character for him, a proud and arrogant man. In *Born Again*, Colson writes that despite his humble origins, he refused to take a full scholarship and a stipend of $50 a month offered by Harvard University, because of "resentment built up over the years to the superior attitude of the whole Harvard academic establishment; the condescension of aristocratic men to those who came out of less fortunate backgrounds." Instead he went to Brown University "which Harvard men looked upon as a poor Ivy League cousin."

Colson's arrogance and ruthlessness soon brought him status and power. He admitted, "I was willing at times to blink at certain ethical standards, to be ruthless in getting things done." It was that reputation which earned him the nickname of Nixon's "hatchet man."

By the time Colson saw the inside of prison he had been knocked down a peg or two—and had learned how to survive in an often hostile environment. Prisoners were a hardened lot, he discovered. The only thing that could turn their lives around, he believed, was knowing Jesus Christ.

Colson discredits any liberal notions of prison reform. "It's just so much liberal humanism to say that it's society's fault that a person commits a crime," he told me. "Over the last 30 years, psychologists and social workers have been saying that crime is the result of poor social and economic conditions, and that prisons exist to rehabilitate criminals. But recent studies have exploded that myth. It is a racist thing to say that more Blacks commit crimes than Whites. In a study of 250 offenders over age 17, it was not race, poverty or the type of crime that was really influential. Changing the prisoners' lifestyles, that was the key factor. That is why conversion to Christianity is so significant. Christian prisoners face their own sin and are accountable for it. There is a danger in saying, 'It's society's fault,' that someone ends up in prison. These people are not victims of society, they are hardened criminals, who must adopt a new lifestyle and make a change."

Colson's motives and methods, and those of other evangelicals, have caused considerable controversy in Canada's hard-pressed prison system.

Reverend Ron Nash, an Anglican priest and chaplain for the Ontario regional headquarters of Correctional Services of Canada counters, "Though the idea is to change the people not the system, I don't think the answer can be only religion. We have to deal with the whole person, his or her psyche, religion and religious roots. I have found in my 15 years here that people's cultural practices and roots have a strong impact on their current situation. And a substantial part of anyone's religion is cultural rather than theological.

"I feel that Colson has a bigoted approach. The evangelical approach, that the *only* way is through Jesus Christ, is not necessarily true. I have met many people who have helped people change in the prisons who are not Christians. The original Greek of the New Testament says that Christianity is *a* way, not *the* way."

But Colson believes that the Prison Fellowship he founded is *the* key. After all, "Only God can change a heart," he says.

Colson has obtained permission from the U.S. Federal Bureau of Prisons to take small groups of Christian inmates out of prison, and send them on a two-week training programme so they can return to custody and minister to other prisoners. During our interview, Colson claimed that not one of the then-300 inmates who had taken the course had contravened the rules of the programme or committed any crime while out of jail. At the end of their two weeks, the inmates are "eager to return to prison as Christ's disciples."

The first six days of the programme consist of intensive study with 16 ordained ministers who have graduate degrees in counselling and psychology. "I have a real problem with lay teachers teaching them," confides Colson. The subjects prisoners study range from theology and Scripture to personal growth. These sessions are held at Ligonier Valley near Pittsburgh. The second week takes place at Holy Name College in Washington, D.C. Every day prisoners listen to a three-hour lecture, and over lunch and dinner at local churches they share testimonies with other Christian activists.

Prison Fellowship also holds in-prison seminars with the full blessing of many prison authorities. The warden at a Nebraska penitentiary told Colson: "Every time you get a convert, we have one less disciplinary problem."

But Reverend Nash is skeptical. "Colson has a glamorous

past and an organization behind him. But we've had community involvement with prisoners for years. Often organizations exist to perpetuate themselves. I think this may be true of the Prison Fellowship."

"One problem I have with them [the Fellowship] is that they come on strong," Nash continues. "Prisoners are in bad shape and often they are looking for a crutch. They can easily be led into the emotionalism of the evangelical movement. I think it is wrong for people to lay this kind of trip on a captive audience. I prefer a foot on the ground approach."

Today Prison Fellowship has a foot firmly in the door in Canadian federal penitentiaries. It began in early 1980 with a phone call from Pierre Allard, another chaplain for the federal prisons, who asked Colson to preach to 80 inmates at Dorchester, New Brunswick. David Farrell, who helped arrange that first meeting, admits, "We are modelling our Fellowship after the U.S. experience."

When I asked Colson if his Fellowship was just another incursion of an American institution into Canada, he was adamant. "The initiative for the Fellowship has come totally from Canadians. Don Yeomans, your commissioner of Correctional Services, welcomed me on my last visit to Collins Bay Penitentiary where I spoke to 150 inmates." On October 9, 1980, Colson and seven board members visited Collins Bay Penitentiary in Kingston to have lunch with a group of Christian prisoners and speak to prisoners in the gymnasium.

Larry Stebbins, assistant warden at Collins Bay, was pleased to see Colson. "I think this Prison Fellowship helps the inmates do time," he said. "They get involved with the prison chaplain and it adds a spiritual dimension to their lives. It also helps them cope with the aggression and drug problems here at the prison."

The five-day seminar that Colson ran at Collins Bay was open to all the inmates. However, Rev. Nash was not impressed. "A lot of people who sell religion do so because of their own needs, perhaps emotional or personality needs. What we always stress to volunteers in the prisons is that they must keep those needs separate from the needs of the people with whom they are working."

"The idea of the Prison Fellowhsip is absolutely foul," counters Claire Culhane, author of *Barred from Prison* and a member of the Vancouver Prisoners' Rights Group. "The problems inmates have in prison won't be solved by any religion. Even Don Yeomans says that 40 percent of those in prisons today don't need to be institutionalized. But what is he doing about it? In my view, this 'born-again' prison group is talking about pie in the sky instead of a union to fight for prison reform."

When confronted with the prison reformers' views Colson laughs belligerently. "Our ministry is committed to reform as well. Reform of the individual. I believe Christianity has a prophetic responsibility for this type of ministry. We have to go into the streets and plant that cross."

In the summer of 1983, Shirley Carr, Paul Hellyer and Leslie Tarr were still on the Canadian executive. Hellyer continues to be enthusiastic about the Fellowship's programme. He says the organization is growing across the country, despite the fact it receives almost no government funding except for small grants for prison seminars. Prison Fellowship has chapters in Vancouver, Edmonton, Calgary, Regina, Toronto, Niagara Falls, Kingston and Ottawa.

One change in the Fellowship is the appointment of a new executive director, Ian Stanley of Mississauga, Ontario, who replaces David Farrell. Farrell, though still active, returned to his job in Ottawa. Stanley previously spent 12 years with World Vision, an evangelical charity organization.

Charles Colson has also maintained his active interest in the Canadian Prison Fellowship, speaking at a Christian Festival in Ottawa in May 1982, and visiting Atlantic Canada as a guest of the Atlantic Baptist Federation in the summer of 1983. While there, Pierre Allard, Chaplain at Dorchester Penitentiary, invited him again. Colson also spoke at the provincial prison in Halifax. Subsequently, Colson and Stanley attended a meeting of Prison Fellowship International in Belfast, Northern Ireland.

Since 1979, Prison Fellowship International—a volunteer ministry designed to "circle the globe"—has been active in Great Britain, Australia, India, the Philippines, Ghana, New Zealand and Japan as well as Canada. Colson is the chairman of the International's board of directors which includes a representative from Jamaica, the wife of a British MP who is also Minister of State for Northern Ireland with jurisdiction for prisons, a U.S. congressman and the president of Youth-for-Christ International.

Nobody can say that Charles Colson isn't ambitious. But then most of the Watergate gang has done well.

# 4
# Home-grown Televangelist

David Mainse smiled kindly at me as we sat in his small, cozy office at 100 Huntley Street.

"So," he began, "my secretary told me you only need a half hour of my time today. She said you want to interview me for a book you're writing on the evangelical movement. I told her that your book sounded mighty important so I might just have to be late for my other appointments.

"Well, Judy Haiven, are you born again?" he asked.

"No, I'm Jewish."

"My, my," gushed Mainse. "One of God's Chosen People. Welcome aboard."

I was becoming used to this. Evangelicals believe that the Jews are God's Chosen People who have a special inheritance from God: Israel. Mainse and other born-again Christians encourage the Jewish people from all over the world to return to Israel. When that happens, the Messiah will return to earth and lift the Christians into heaven. This happens to fit neatly into prevailing Zionist views—calling for Jews around the world to settle permanently in Israel—and goes a long way to explaining the personal friendship between Menachem Begin, the former Israeli prime minister, and Falwell.

Under Begin, and his successor, Yitzhak Shamir, U.S. evangelists have enjoyed special status in Israel. For instance, American evangelist George Otis owns a radio station in

Israel; the government allows the station to proselytize over the airwaves in return for broadcasting "Voice of Israel" news casts. Jimmy Swaggart, gospel singer and Louisiana-based TV evangelist, explains, "I feel that America is tied with the spiritual umbilical cord to Israel. The ties go back long before the founding of the United States of America. The Judeo-Christian concept goes all the way back to Abraham and God's promise to Abraham which I believe also included America."

In Mainse's autobiography, *100 Huntley Street*, he explains his desire to befriend a Jewish shopkeeper in Chalk River where Mainse taught school years ago. A Jewish girl in his class, Sandra Levine, had a father who ran the general store. Mr. Levine liked to play chess, so Mainse learned how to play and "would play with him during quiet afternoons in the store—occasionally taking the opportunity to share a little about the Messiah with him." But Mainse was disappointed; though they became good friends, "I had not succeeded in having him receive his Messiah."

David Mainse, born in 1936, spent his early years on a farm near Ramsayville, just outside of Ottawa. "We were very poor in those days, but I didn't know it. There was always enough to eat and always fresh vegetables from our garden....We had to make do on the five dollars a week the missionary board paid us."

Mainse's father, Rev. Roy L. Mainse, was a missionary from "The Holiness Movement," an offshoot of 50 congregations of the Methodists, that later merged with the Free Methodists partly due to the elder Mainse's activities. He spent most of David's childhood in Asyet, Egypt. Mainse's mother and two older sisters raised him in a four-room addition to the farmhouse owned by his Uncle Harvey and Aunt Mina. Because of the outbreak of the Second World War, Rev. Mainse was not able to return home until 1944—after six years in Egypt. As his son wrote later, "He could do nothing but consign his family into the Lord's hands while he was about his Father's business, and trust that God would take care of us."

Mainse learned to read at five and attended a one-room school presided over by a terrifying but apparently inspiring Miss Bice. His description of growing up a missionary's son in rural Ontario is almost a cliche.

When his father was appointed principal of Annesley College, the Mainse family moved to Ottawa where the ten-year-old David became a go-fer for the Ottawa Roughriders, and began demonstrating the perhaps disturbing entrepreneurial talent that has sparked his later career. Mainse's mother died of cancer, his father remarried, returned to Egypt and left Mainse a boarder at Brockville Bible College. Motorcycling and other forms of rebellion ended with Mainse giving his life to Christ at a Youth for Christ rally in Ottawa, leaving his father's church for the Pentecostal church and eventually for the Eastern Pentecostal Bible College in Peterborough. While still a student, he ministered in Chalk River and Brighton, Ontario, and met and married his wife Norma-Jean. During his first call, to Deep River, parishioners responded to his characteristic drive and enthusiasm.

Family ties resulted in Mainse's TV debut with Norma-Jean's two brothers, the "King's Men," on the Pembroke station—at 11:30 on a Saturday night in 1962 at a cost of $55. Calls jammed the switchboard and Mainse never looked back. The one-shot appearance became a weekly show and when Mainse moved with his growing family to Sudbury, the congregation had to agree to take the TV show too. The Pembroke station became Mainse's first syndication: the manager called Sudbury and asked for a tape. Now called Crossroads, it soon spread to Sault Ste. Marie, Timmins, North Bay, Quebec City, Toronto, Vancouver and Montreal.

It was at this time that Mainse had two inspirations (credited, in his book, to St. Paul). The telecasts were not supporting themselves through random viewer's donations: hence, prayer partners were needed who would make regular monthly contributions along with their prayers. Also, Mainse had a "picture in my mind's eye of telephones, with people calling in, right while we were on the air, to commit their lives to Christ or to ask for healing. . . ." A year later, as Mainse pointed out, Pat Robertson developed the concept which would result in The 700 Club.

In 1968, the Mainse family moved to Bethel Church in Hamilton. Crossroads was produced in colour in Kitchener. In August 1970, Mainse took the big plunge: he left his growing church for full-time television.

In 1972 Mainse gambled—and won, bringing his show to prime time and national attention. Crossroads, in syndication, was playing on 25 or so stations. He planned a Grey Cup Christian Celebration in all the major TV markets for the week after Grey Cup, hiring the McMaster gymnasium and assembling a huge cast and crew. Contributions eventually covered expenses and according to Mainse, "The cumulative impact was immeasurable. It changed a lot of people's thinking about the relevance and impact of national Christian television. . . ."

Maine's office, smaller and more modest than I had expected, is barely ten feet square. Old, patched shag broadloom hugs the floor and dark wooden bookshelves line one wall. His 1950s vintage semi-circular desk is flanked by two low slung chairs and a couch that could be 30 years old.

After the opulence of Pat Robertson's 700 Club "spread" in Virginia Beach, and the ersatz colonial grandeur of Jerry Falwell's Thomas Road Baptist Church, I was surprised when I walked into the modest two-storey red-brick building at 100 Huntley Street.

The office was so small in fact, that from any chair I could see the titles of some of the books on his shelves. Darwin's *The Origin of Species* sat next to Hal Lindsay's bestselling book on Bible prophecy *The Late Great Planet Earth*. The former Florida orange juice queen's autobiography, *The Anita Bryant Story*, was on a shelf with a smattering of general interest books on public speaking, sociology and travelogues about the Holy Land. Little mementoes from Mainse's preaching abroad cluttered the desk; an Aboriginal boomerang, a sculpture of praying hands.

On my way into Mainse's office, I had noticed the Right to Life anti-abortion poster, banned by the Toronto transit system, pinned to the wall. The controversial, but brilliantly executed, poster shows a colourful toy tin soldier with a big tear rolling down his face. The poster reads, "This Christmas there will be fewer children to play with the toys."

I asked Mainse if he supported the Right to Life Association. "No, that was put up by our filmmaker, Bruce Allen. He and his wife are strong Right-to-Lifers," Mainse explained. "We believe that the taking of any human life is wrong. For instance, the people who are anti-capital punishment but pro-abortion are using faulty logic. These people want to protect the life of the murderers.

"When you think it through logically, it is the lack of value for human life right across the board, the lack of value for the victim's life that causes a person to treat murder as if it is no more serious a crime than knocking over a jewellery store. You'll get the same amount of time in jail, after all, and time off for good behaviour. When someone has to forfeit his own life for taking another person's life, you are placing the highest possible value on human life."

"But a life is a life," I said, "an eye for an eye justice doesn't really uphold your view of the sanctity of life. Isn't any taking of life murder?"

Mainse went on, "I believe that capital punishment is a deterrent. The Scriptures teach that the government, the law, is a terror to those who do wrong. The government has a responsibility for judicious execution. When a person who has taken another human being's life is killed, that person forfeits his own right to live. That is not murder."

Mainse, earnest and polite, leaned forward to emphasize

**Jeannie C. Riley**

**Jimmy Swaggart**

**Bob MacDougall**

**Arthur Blessitt**

**Chuck Colson**

**Donna Douglas**

*Above*: 100 Huntley Street guest stars. *Left*: On the set of the French-language Au Centuple show. *Right*: The studio crew at work. *Opposite page*: Excerpts from a David Mainse fundraising letter.

100 Huntley Street, Toronto, Ontario M4Y 2L1
Telephone Bus. (416) 961-8001
Prayer and Counselling 961-1800

CROSSROADS

*I've never written a letter like this before. this is the most urgent one ever!*

May 5, 1982

Dear Partner:

What can I say, except that I feel a great love for you. You have been the great extension of God's loving heart to this Ministry. Now I must come to you again. I know you would want me to, and my Board has asked me to. God has blessed for 20 years since Crossroads first went on TV. It's eight years since Circle Square began blessing our children and five years on June 15th since 100 Huntley Street started. As of this date over 750,000 calls have come to our 27 counselling centres across Canada. Multiplied thousands have made first-time decisions for Christ, and thousands more have been reclaimed and blessed in many ways. Homes and churches have been helped. I could share much more, but you know the effectiveness of this work. Otherwise, you wouldn't have supported us already.

*Important*

Please give your best gift right away. We could even take care of this crisis by the fifth birthday of 100 Huntley Street on June 15th if we all participate. Also encourage your friends to help.

We just won't be here without you. I've just prayed fervently and asked God to tell me an amount each one should give, and He won't let me. He says again, "My sheep know my voice." PLEASE, PLEASE, ask Him now what He wants you to do and then trust Him for that amount that comes into your thoughts. I believe that still small voice tells me now that unusually large amounts (as far as regular giving patterns are concerned) will be given and that the Holy Spirit will be faithful to speak to everyone who receives this.

Again, let me assure you that, whatever happens, I love you with all my heart.

Your Brother and Partner,

David

David Mainse
President

the next point. I didn't pick up the animosity in his tone of voice until I went home and listened to the tape. Face-to-face Mainse's charm was so compelling, I hardly noticed the chill in his answer.

"In the case of an abortion, there are all kinds of people cooperating to take that little life that has done no wrong, committed no crime and deserves to live in this society. At 100 Huntley Street we don't go running around espousing causes because that is not our calling; our mandate is simply to proclaim the gospel of Christ."

Mainse further emphasized his point, "As a young man of 16 I really believed that the Lord spoke to me, not in an audible voice, but it was very real to me. God called me to proclaim the Word. That's *my* calling in life. I don't go running around espousing causes because that is *not* my calling."

I reminded him that a year before I had seen Geoffrey Shaw, one of the leading Huntley Street staff, speak on a platform for a new political party, The Moderate Moral Majority—which is now defunct.

"Oh, that was something he did on his own, as a private citizen. Organizations are always taking advantage of people in our ministry like that. I will never get involved in something like a Moral Majority. But I will seek to see that the lives of doctors who perform abortions, politicians or judges, have their lives redirected in the faith of God."


Although Mainse professes the utmost respect and admiration for the U.S. evangelical shows like The PTL Club and The 700 Club, he claims he had been assured by their hosts that neither show would be broadcast in Canada and the airwaves would be free for the advent of Huntley Street. But both U.S. TV ministries subsequently did come to Canada, and he is quick to wave the Canadian flag when it is to his advantage. Mainse says, "I was shocked when it happened, but almost immediately I saw God's hand in what had happened to us. Now I understood why we had such a sense of urgency to get the programme on the air . . . Clearly, God intended Canada to have its own voice and witness."

Mainse insists the major difference between Huntley Street and the U.S. shows is that his co-hosts come from many Christian denominations, including Pentecostal, Catholic, Anglican, United Church, Baptist and Free Methodist. Mainse adds, "It does seem to be a fulfillment of the prayer of Jesus: 'When they see that they are one, they will believe, Father, that you sent me.' For 100 Huntley Street may well be the most visible expression of unity in the body of Christ in our nation today."

100 Huntley Street is broadcast throughout Canada on 26 stations and on over 450 cable stations in the United States. R. Russell Bixler, president of WPCB-TV in Pittsburgh, Pennsylvania, is quoted on the back of Mainse's autobiography as saying: "WPCB-TV is the first U.S. television station to carry this Canadian programme, and it has left its American viewers somewhat breathless. David and his programme convey a gentle excitement, a gracious warmth, and a definite annointing of God's spirit."

As a fellow evangelical, Bixler's words of praise are, of course, exaggerated. But it is true that Mainse and his show are *qualitatively* different from similar U.S. shows.

100 Huntley Street is just the tip of the iceberg. Its Christian Multilingual Programming (CMP) produces programmes in five languages which serve non-English speaking Canadians and Americans and are exported to Europe and South America.

According to a brochure, these TV programmes are "designed to share Jesus Christ and His power to save, heal, baptize and bless in these days." Most are aired on Toronto's Multilingual Channel 47, which exacts $1375 for every hour of air time.

*Au 100 Tuple* is a French-language one-hour show broadcast only in Sherbrooke and Trois-Rivieres, though it is produced in Toronto at the Huntley Street studios.

CMP also produces a half-hour show in Ukrainian (Our Hope) which is aired twice a week in Toronto and Lloydminster, Alberta. Their German show, Ein Erfulltes Leben, will soon be seen on cable in Switzerland.

A church in Toronto's Greek Community sacrificed its building plans to support a Greek evangelical TV ministry and was rewarded "when the Lord gave them their own church building." CMP produces a one-hour show in Greek (Zondas 100 Tiz 100) which is seen in Toronto and in Pittsburgh.

The Italian show, Vivere al 100 Per Cento, is seen on 17 stations in Canada and the U.S. as well as throughout Italy. There are 20 Italian telephone counselling centres.

Portugal and Brazil are mission targets in addition to Toronto for Vida Cem Per Cento, a Portuguese telecast from Huntley Street.

In addition to the multilingual programming, Huntley Street produces a telecast for the deaf, Sign of the Times, and a popular "pre-evangelistic" children's show, Circle Square. Huntley Street, however, rarely has to purchase air time for these two because they are usually classed as public service shows, and they help stations meet their quota for Canadian content.

The Circle Square programmes, and the enthusiasm of one of Norma-Jean Mainse's brothers, Reynald Rutledge, gave birth to the Circle Square Ranch ministry on donated farms. In 1983, five ranches—at Halkirk, Alberta, Severn Bridge, Ontario, Arden, Ontario, 100 Mile House, British Columbia, and Sussex, New Brunswick—offer a children's camp in a Christian setting, at about half the cost of similar camps.

Mainse has also created Mainroads Productions Inc., which produces and distributes books, records and educational materials. There are about 40 records and tapes, including albums by Norma-Jean Mainse, who sings on the show, her brothers—Glen and Reynald Rutledge—and Mainse's daughter and son-in-law, Elaine and Bruce Stacey.

The "Stacey" albums are reportedly very popular with young people since they combine the easy listening rock music with the all-important born-again message. Bruce Stacey writes both lyrics and music; this one is called "So Many Writers."

*Lord, if the song's not from my heart*
*Never let me start*
*Bind my hands that I may never play*
*I may never play . . .*
*It's so nice to grab a catchy phrase*
*Like maybe "Jesus Saves" or "Alleluja"*
*Never let these become*
*Just words to sing.*
*But let my love for Thee*
*Flow naturally in my songs.*

Mainroads produces *The Stacey Music Book* and *Only the Children Know* music books so listeners at home can learn to play the words and music to two of the Stacey albums.

David Mainse narrates a teaching cassette kit, Crossroads Creation Series, which includes six teaching cassettes and a study guide for the *alternative* to Darwin theory, Creationism. The kit, which costs $29.95, has reportedly been bought by school boards.

Mainse comments, "The reason we did that 13-week television series on Crossroads, Science and the Bible, is because schools are so over-balanced on the side of Evolution. My one son, who had just finished grade 13, received the top award in his high school in biology. He brought that Creationism series into his teacher. The teacher looked at it and said, 'This is what I've been wanting for years. I never heard anybody or read anything on the Creation side that was the least bit scientific.'

"For example, the age of the earth. Carbon datings go right

along with the Scripture; they are within the parameters of Scriptural time, the genealogies that go back through the Jews, Abraham, Noah, Enoch and Adam. Isaac Asimov, the great American science writer, said there would be 17 feet of dust on the moon because according to his calculations, the moon has been there so many *millions* of years. Walter Cronkite asked the astronaut Armstrong how much dust there was on the moon. Armstrong said it was only *scuff deep!* You know how much dust that was? Only from six to ten *thousand* years of dust on the moon! Of course, Asimov has not referred to it since," Mainse reported with obvious relish.

"You know what I used to do before I talked to these creation scientists? I went through all kinds of mental gymnastics to work these *millions* of years into my theory of how God created the earth. Boy, these scientists made a *convert* out of *me.* You've heard of the KISS theory? Keep it Simple Stupid. That's what it says and that's what I believe."

Mainroads has published four books to date. Diane Roblin Lee, a staff member at Huntley Street, is the author of *My Father's Child*, about growing up with a father who is a minister. She was resentful of her father because he neglected his family in order to minister to others; she was resentful of other children in the congregation who got more attention than she did and she was resentful toward God. "I wanted to go to the dances, and I wanted to go to the shows, and play cards and go out with boys and do all the things I saw my friends doing. I didn't have the help of the Holy Spirit to take that appeal of the world away from me...." Naturally, as she started to write, "The Lord just healed all of those memories, and took all of that garbage out....I went through university living totally as a Humanist, and after university, I married and we had two young children." Lee's marriage was falling apart and she tried transcendental meditation and transactional analysis but "there was always something lacking." Finally, her mother and aunt fasted and prayed for her every Monday and it wasn't long before she started to read her Bible. Three months after she accepted the Lord, her husband did as well.

Now Lee edits and writes *The Mainroads Record*, the company's promotional magazine. Another Mainroads title is *Child of Woe*, by Maury Blair, a personal story of rejection and degradation at the hands of his mother and stepfather. Then after 19 years "God confronted him with the reality of Himself" through a book by Dr. Norman Vincent Peale called *Stay Alive All of Your Life*. Blair is now head of Teen Challenge, an evangelical mission to teenagers in Toronto. When a young, lonely youth tells Blair he's had a raw deal, Blair writes, "I can tell him to quit feeling sorry for himself and just give God an opportunity to work....God can change lives and He'll do the same thing for anyone who will believe."

*Canada: Sharing our Christian Heritage* is a large format quality paperback in colour that presents Canadian history, again from an evangelical viewpoint. All of these publications are advertised on Huntley Street and featured in the Huntley bookshop off the cafeteria.

In 1983, the CRTC agreed to license a new satellite cable TV service for a broadly based interfaith network and called for proposals. The new network, according to the CRTC, must undertake to present a balanced view of religion and to reflect the various religious denominations in Canada.

Wendell Wilks, assistant to David Mainse, was delighted by the news. "We are working with Interchurch Communications, a cooperative body which represents five Protestant groups and the Catholic Church. We are ready to share our research and our technical expertise with them." The Metropolitan (Toronto) Interfaith Cable TV Association, which includes non-Christian church groups, is also expected to be involved. However on a recent call-in show in

Toronto (Radio-Noon) Mainse refused to say that in his opinion groups other than Christians and Jews would be welcome and continually referred to the prospective network as "Christian."

Reverend Randy Naylor, secretary, Division of Communications of the United Church of Canada, explains that the Canadian Interfaith Network already includes the United Church, Anglican Church, Lutheran churches, Greek Orthodox, Salvation Army, Christian Reformed, a consortium of Baptists and 100 Huntley Street. Buddhist, Moslem and Zoroastrian faiths are also part of the Network. The Roman Catholic and Jewish religions have yet to join.

Each religion has to buy one share of the Network—a guarantee that it will fund twelve hours per year of prime-time, which includes production of shows. The Network itself is considering a two-hour nightly programme of news, commentary and entertainment with an ecumenical slant, tentatively called Cornerstone.

The Network's initial commitment is for a 16-hour television day, eventually to be extended to 24 hours. In addition to the idea of members owning shares and producing their own shows, they are encouraged to buy more air time. Naylor sees the Network as commercially viable but not for profit, and ultimately employing 150 people. It will also accept advertising that "values the person"—that is consistent with Network values. In an effort to give the Network a boost, there may be a joint nation-wide fundraising appeal to get the station on the air.

"Ninety-two percent of Canadians have some relationship to the Deity," says Rev. Naylor. "More Canadians attend church service on one Sunday than attend a sports event once a year. We have a real community base from which to work. I think the kind of people interested in Man Alive [on CBC-TV Sunday nights] will watch us. And one million people watch Man Alive. Our research indicates four million viewers a week will watch a religious network."

While the CRTC took a dim view of raising money

through "pitches," as the evangelicals are now doing, the door is open to other forms of fundraising, such as selling memberships to the Network, telephone soliciting and raising money the way Public Broadcasting does in the U.S.

In the current climate of economic constraint, Crossroads has had to cut back on the purchase of air time. Other denominations and churches have not moved to undertake the necessary production and air time costs. The decision by the CRTC will allow the churches to produce and air programmes of common concern, including news, public affairs, and even denominational programming, at what is hoped will be a fraction of current costs. The hearing before the CRTC is anticipated in mid-November 1984.

# 5
## "God Don't Sponsor No Fluff"

"At every meeting we have an alter call," warned Jim McEwen on the phone, "and God may call on you to be baptized in the Holy Spirit." McEwen, an evangelist and Toronto public relations man, had reserved a seat for me at the Full Gospel Businessmen's Fellowship Ontario Convention.

Driving up the ramp of the three-storey parking garage by the hotel at 7:00 a.m., I noticed it was packed and that nearly every car sported a bumper sticker: "Jesus: He's the Answer"; "Have a Good Day with Jesus"; and "Happiness is Sharing Jesus." I knew I was in the right place.

In a large ballroom at the Constellation Hotel on Toronto's "airport strip," hundreds of men and women and a sprinkling of children sat patiently at scores of linen-covered tables waiting for breakfast to begin. Most of the men wore three-piece suits and ties; the women were decked out in their Sunday best; the kids practically gleamed from scrubbing. There was hardly an empty seat in the hall, which accommodates 900 people. An usher took me to a front row table and sat me down with smiling strangers. Everyone at the table had brought his own Bible, usually in a leatherette case with several bookmarks drooping out of the pages.

As I sat down, I heard several of my tablemates discussing a prophecy. "Well," the skinny man with the glasses explained to me, "though we do discuss certain parts of the Bible, we all believe the Bible is the unerring word of God—from cover to cover. After all, God's word is truth." The argument broke off and eight heads bobbed approvingly.

I nodded uncomfortably and thought of Lot's wife. Had she really turned into a pillar of salt, I wondered aloud? The man across the table who had first answered was suspicious. "Of course. Every word is the truth. Remember that."

The rest of my table had slipped patiently into the long line for the buffet breakfast and I was left to face my "teacher." "Oh, I always did want to know what the real story was," I joked. "Now you have it," said the man with the glasses somewhat sharply.


The Full Gospel Businessmen's Fellowship, Inc., Dallas, Texas, was founded in 1952 by Demos Shakarian, an Armenian-American land developer and rancher in Downey, California. The Fellowship has 2200 chapters in 70 countries around the world, including 200 chapters in Canada. Seventy or so of them are in Ontario and ten are in Quebec, seven of which are French-speaking.

"We have lots of Protestants and Catholics coming to meetings," explained the regional coordinator, Jim Hatton, in a phone interview. "We are truly interdenominational and we have members from over 59 denominations. I'm a member of the United Church and even my minister is a member of the Fellowship."

Membership, open only to men, costs a mere $20 a year, which helps support the five-man national office in Malton, Ontario where Hatton works. "It is true that membership is open only to men but we use the term 'businessmen' in the larger sense of the word. We actually mean laymen, rather than clergymen.

"Women are welcome to come to meetings, prayer

breakfasts or dinners, but can't join." According to Hatton, there are over 5000 members across the country and the Fellowship is growing every day.

What do they do? Each chapter meets once a month either for a prayer breakfast on a Saturday or a week night dinner to share testimony, praise the Lord, and collect "offerings" that finance the Fellowship's outreach programmes. Their outreach programmes range from a prison ministry to buying and shipping Bibles to faraway lands and to hosting banquets that honour the local police.

Hatton, a former community college chemistry and mathematics teacher, boasted, "We have converted the President of Honduras, the prime ministers of Guyana and Belize, and the Minister of the Interior for Nicaragua, to born-again Christianity. Tomas Borge, the Nicaraguan Minister of the Interior, was a Sandinista and was tortured by Somoza's men. His wife and daughter were raped and then murdered by those men. But since then, Borge has accepted Jesus Christ as his Lord and Saviour and has gone into the prisons of Managua to help others find the Lord. One day Borge came across the man who had raped and killed his family and do you know what Borge said to him? He told that murderer, 'I forgive you.' Though there is still a lot of hate in that country, people are changing. A swimming pool has just been built in the prison for baptisms. Over 700 prisoners have been baptized. . . .

"You've probably also heard that the Cubans are helping rebuild that country that was torn apart by the war. Well, do you know what book they are using to teach the people to read and write? They are using the Bibles that we supplied. We sent 100,000 last year and we are now printing over 700,000 in Spanish for Nicaragua. We give them away.

"Our ministry has met with Indira Ghandi. She invited us to come back to India any time. Her personal secretary has accepted Christ."

The Full Gospel's work is not confined to the international arena. Their publication *Set Free* details the conversions of many prisoners in Canadian institutions. Darryl Gellner, 31 and convicted of two murders, is an inmate of Collins Bay penitentiary. In *Set Free* he writes about his conversion: "One change that happened right away was the calmness and peace that swept over me, feelings that I wouldn't trade for all the money in the world. Those feelings have continued. In fact, as I write these lines from a prison cell, I feel more free than I did on the outside. You can't know that peace and freedom until you trust Jesus."

Gellner and James Cavanaugh, another inmate at Collins Bay, hold Bible Study meetings and prayer study in cells at the penitentiary.

"They may be considered more quickly when their parole time comes around," said Hatton, "and in fact in January, both men are getting day releases to come down to Toronto to appear on 100 Huntley Street to give their testimony."

The Full Gospel Businessmen's Fellowship was also producing a half-hour TV show called Good News, featuring two testimonials on each programme, at the Global Television studios in Toronto. The Fellowship paid for studio and editing time but not the guests on the show. "In three days we shoot 13 shows," Hatton told me, "and we have even done TV specials on prime-time TV. In 1975, one of our prime-time specials earned us an Emmy Award."

From 1977-82, Good News was marketed around the world. A copy of each half-hour tape was made for Canadian audiences and for chapters across the United States which sponsored airings on local U.S. stations.

Hatton explained that though the shows were not currently being aired in Ontario, they were shown on western stations often just before or after the late-night national news "when a lot of people watch, but when it costs only a little to buy air time." As recently as 1982, Good News was shown in Saskatoon, Edmonton, Kelowna, Kamloops, Regina and Calgary.

Good News has shown on 2932 stations across the U.S., has run on the Far Eastern Broadcasting Network to the

Philippines, and has been translated for Japanese and Chinese audiences. In 1980 it was shown on 70 channels in each of Australia and New Zealand. In Europe it was carried on radio. Kenya gave the Fellowship free air time so the only cost was mailing it to Africa from international headquarters in the U.S. "People can write in when they see the shows, or phone a local number for prayer counselling," noted Hatton.

The show has been suspended for the past year. The Full Gospel Businessmen's Fellowship is waiting for completion of their new television studios in Costa Mesa, California before they resume production.

In June 1980, 47 members of the fellowship in Canada and the U.S. visited China for 16 days. "We just went to find out what was happening there," explained Hatton, "and what we found out was that people were free to pray in centres like Canton and Shanghai and they were allowed to practise their religion. One man on our tour who spoke Chinese translated the sermon given at a local service and it was just like a Christian sermon anywhere else.

"We're not anti-Communist, or anti-Capitalist. We're Pro-God."

Hatton told me that one of their international directors actually sat down to meals with generals from El Salvador who had thrown children up in the air for target practice. "Even members of the ruling junta have proclaimed their faith."

Isn't that kind of a contradiction?

"Well, it *is* a contradiction," he admitted, "but as their faith grows they will apply it to their own lives. Proclaiming their faith is the first step."


My right hand absently slopped the coffee onto the saucer as I watched my tablemates finish their breakfasts, push away their plates and plant their Bibles in place of the dishes. The keynote speaker stood up at the head table.

"When you take God out of the schools, Satan comes in," warned Ben Kinchlow, popular TV evangelist and co-host of The 700 Club. On the show, Kinchlow seems to be the common man's interpreter and sidekick to the more sophisticated Pat Robertson.

Pat Robertson, the Dick Cavett of television evangelists, is a Yale Law School graduate and son of a former U.S. senator. Robertson is the president and founder of the Christian Broadcasting Network, which grew out of the U.S.'s first Christian TV station which he started in 1961. By 1980, the CBN included four TV stations, 200 affiliate stations, six radio stations, a missionary recording company, a programme service for 3000 cable systems, a news network and a university, to quote the press booklets from Washington for Jesus in which Robertson played a major role. He boasts more than 7000 telephone counsellors.

Noted for its expertise in satellite communications, the CBN was the first Christian organization in the U.S. to own and operate a satellite earth station.

Robertson holds court for 90 minutes daily with born-again guests who represent virtually every walk of life in the U.S. today, but the show is heavily loaded with entertainers and politicians. His political pontifications range from condemning the American Civil Liberties Union for being anti-God to railing against the Equal Rights Amendment.

I had first run across Kinchlow at the Washington for Jesus rally, a year-and-a-half before. In answer to the media's accusation that the rally was a fundamentalist public relations stunt, Kinchlow had bellowed, "God don't sponsor no fluff," to 175,000 born agains in Washington's Mall.

A month later I visited the headquarters of the Christian Broadcasting Network (CBN) in Virginia Beach, Virginia, a resort town on the Atlantic near Norfolk. I got a first-hand look at what is the most modern broadcasting facility in the United States. CBN had nearly reached its goal of becoming the fourth largest network in the U.S. (after the "majors,"

*Top*: The Christian Broadcasting Network's headquarters in Virginia Beach, Virginia. *Below*: Phone banks at The 700 Club. Viewers call in for prayer and counselling.

*Top*: Sporting white bucks, singer Pat Boone stands in for host Pat Robertson on The 700 Club. That day's theme was the 1950s. *Below*: CBN University's graduate school for communications, adjacent to the main CBN building.

NBC, ABC and CBS). The 700 Club, CBN's biggest drawing card, is their big money-maker.

An immense modern facility set amidst manicured lawns, it looks like an antebellum plantation-owner's mansion. A vast pillared portico is flanked by two wings which contain the broadcast studios.

The immense lobby is furnished only with 18th century-style console tables. It is overlooked by bronze figurines on a raised platform depicting heroes of the Revolutionary War.

I was met by Ethel Steadman, a public relations officer who was to be my guide. Everything was expensive and very, very new. Robertson wasn't on stage that day as I sat in the studio audience of The 700 Club—Pat Boone was the guest host and the theme was the 1950s.

The CBN's plans for the near future included 24-hour-a-day "Christian alternative" programming including situation comedies, soap operas—one tentatively named "The Inner Light"—news casts and children's shows.

But as far as my guide was concerned, personal testimony and conversion were the aim of Christian television. "I used to be a 'secular humanist' just like you," said Ethel Steadman, "then I accepted Jesus as my personal Lord and Savior and I quit working for the local newspaper [the *Virginia-Pilot*] and am devoting my life to Him." This was a common refrain. Several others told me they had left responsible and high-paying jobs in the secular media to take jobs at CBN at a fraction of their former salaries. They radiated energy and enthusiasm.

According to Steadman, it is a constant challenge to find Americans in public life who have been born again and want to give their testimony. "We get hundreds of letters every week from people across the country asking if they can give testimony on The 700 Club but we are looking for people whose lives have been turned around and dramatically changed by becoming born again."

Her hottest prospect at the time was song-writer and 1960s

rebel Bob Dylan. "We know his pastor out in California, who is pastor to many stars. We know he goes to Bible Study twice a week and is changing his life. If we got him to give his testimony it would be a real coup."

A black man with a wry sense of humour, Ben Kinchlow seems an unlikely co-host for a ministry of the air. He is over six feet tall, with a build like a football player. The day I interviewed him, he sported a natty double-breasted navy blazer with shiny metal buttons, a navy and red striped tie, grey pants and a gold-coloured 700 Club lapel pin. Kinchlow tried to inject a little fun into the grey sameness of the assembled businessmen. "I know all you out there are Christians," thundered Kinchlow to the crowd of 800 Full Gospel Businessmen and their families after breakfast. "But how many of you think: I might be in the body of Christ but I'm not significant? I'm worse than a toenail; I'm just a corn!" Roars of laughter.

"But that's the wrong way to think. You should be thinking, 'I am one of the redeemed of the Lord. I don't have to live a life under fear, defeat, frustration, and sickness under the heel of Satan.' You see, God never called us to live *under* the circumstances; he called us to be *overcomers!*"

"'Overcomers,' that's right," whispered the bright-eyed, middle-aged woman who sat beside me. My attention was divided between her and the speaker.

"Do you know something?" she whispered. "I overcame cancer at one of these Full Gospel breakfasts a year ago. Really. And God has provided me with whatever I've needed over the years. For instance, my eldest son died of kidney disease a few months ago. We didn't know where we'd even get the money to bury him, seeing as my husband is on pension. But the Lord came through. Money started arriving in the mail—$10 here and $50 there. No names, no thanks asked for. We had enough money and more besides. As the

Bible says, God gives us according to our needs, not our greeds!"

As I tried to shift my view back to the stage and Kinchlow, she caught my eye. "What about you, are you born again?" But before I had time to reply, she answered her own question. "Well. Ask me all the questions you want, dear, and maybe by the end of the day we'll have another convert to Christ."


Kinchlow continued.

"You know what accounts for the difference between the way you looked at 6:00 a.m. today and the way you look now?" A titter ran through the audience. "The way you look now is the direct result of the efforts you spent at the mirror earlier. Now ladies: say Amen, and do I hear the men saying, 'Thank God!'"

More laughter.

"You have to have the faith to believe that God provides miracles and everyone that has even a little bit must exercise it regularly. To him that . . ."

"Has!" yelled out the audience.

"Will more be . . ."

"Given!" The crowd finished his sentence.

The assembly was like a classroom of kids as Kinchlow entreated the audience to complete his sentences.


"If God says it; that's the way it—

"IS," shouted the audience.

"Give and it shall be given to you."

"Luke 6:38," the crowd replied.


"If we believed that," smiled Kinchlow, "we'd give with a shovel rather than a tiny McDonald's spoon. Now, turn to the lady right next to you—if that's your wife—and say,

'Honey, you've made my life beautiful, but you're getting a little chunky.'"

Whoops of laughter from the floor.

"Scientists have asked me, 'How can an intelligent man like yourself accept the theory of creation?' It's easy, I say, I know the Creator."

Thunderous applause and a standing ovation.

The sermon ended, it was time for Kinchlow to pray for the faithful.

"Praise the Lord," said the portly man who sat at my left elbow as he shook my hand. Joe was a superintendent of a large suburban apartment building. "Let me tell you what happened to me. I'm from Leamington, Ontario, and I used to be a farmer. Well, the season hadn't gone well and my wife and I were worried about how we could even keep food on the table for our three children. My wife had just sent our last $50 to Billy Graham. We prayed and prayed and knew that God would answer our prayers. One day, we had to go into town and when we returned our eldest son ran over to the truck. He waved an envelope addressed to me. 'This just came in the mail,' he told me. I opened it and found ten hundred-dollar bills. $1000! No return address, no postmark, no nothing. God sure does meet our needs!"

"Hallelujah, Praise the Lord," chirped the others at the table.

"Do you know why this is the *Full* Gospel Businessmen's Fellowship?" he asked me. I shook my head. "Some churches only believe in one part or another or they tell you some of the Bible was just stories—not the word of God. Well that's what we call Sunday Christians. We believe every word is the word of God."

At that moment Kinchlow launched into prayer.

Joe stared at the stage in admiration.

"If God says I'm all right, *I'm AWRIGHT!*" Kinchlow told his fans. "Don't let the Devil steal anything from you. Turn away from lust—I know there is a man out there who has a problem with lust," looking at the audience, "but just walk away from it...There's a woman in the centre of this room who's had a hard time with shin splints. Please heal her God. A few older people in this assembly with colitis—I know it's hard for you. Please heal them, God. One man to my left has cancer. And a young woman has a scar that won't heal. Jesus, I'm praying for you to help them."

The woman at my side squeezed my hand and smiled.

Ulcers, colitis, emphysema and more; what affliction wasn't mentioned, wasn't prayed about? Organ music playing softly in the background, everyone rising to say a final prayer, arms stretched toward the ceiling, eyes closed tightly. Afterwards, Kinchlow announced he'd be glad to pray with anyone who needed his services. A line began to form from the podium, down the platform steps and into the crowd.

I tried to figure out what I had to do to get a personal interview with Kinchlow.

All of a sudden, I felt strong arms around my shoulders. An older man peeked around at me.

It was Bob Jackson, the ambulance driver I'd met on the bus ride to Washington for Jesus. "God has made me rich today. Imagine seeing you here. It's wonderful, a real miracle. I'd hoped that I'd see you again but I thought it would be"—his eyes rose heavenward—"a while from now. How are you?"

I was glad to see a friendly face and told him so.

"You look so good," he gushed, "I just want to hold you tight." He gave me a bear hug. "In fact what I'd really like to do to you should be downright illegal!" His eyes glistened with tears as he introduced me to some of his friends. "May God bless you and your lucky husband," he told me. With one last hug, he crushed a business card into my palm, waved goodbye and headed for the private counselling room.

When I finally did buttonhole Kinchlow, the banquet hall was noisy with preparations for the convention's luncheon. Amid the clatter of trays and dishes and the trickle of ice and water filling 800 glasses, Kinchlow and I sat down for the interview.

From the brochures I had collected from my tour to the Christian Broadcasting Network in Virginia Beach, Ben Kinchlow seemed like an unlikely convert to Christ.

Texas-born and raised, he enrolled in Southwest Texas Junior College under the GI Bill after 13 years with the U.S. Air Force as a non-commissioned officer. He made the Dean's list and was even named in the *Who's Who in Small Colleges*.

While at school he worked part-time as a test car driver and a car salesman and made about $12,000 a year—part-time. "Not bad for a college student," says Kinchlow.

In 1969, Kinchlow found God when he was driving a test car around a track at 80 miles per hour. "I was listening to a top 40 station on the radio, smoking a cigarette and lo and behold, out of my mouth this old spiritual started. I immediately put a stop to that," he wrote, "but it started again, and I stopped it again. I think I started cursing. Then it started a third time."

Before his conversion, Kinchlow had been a disciple of Black Muslim Malcolm X. When Malcolm X was assassinated, he turned to Jesus. "I felt like he might have been a good man and probably believed what he was talking about," Kinchlow wrote of Malcolm X, "but the best he could do was to get himself killed. Man, I didn't need some dead dude telling me how to get killed! I wanted somebody to tell me how to live."

After accepting Christ, Kinchlow began work helping young people kick the drug habit on a Christian farm in Killeen, Texas. From there, with Elijah-like swiftness, he rose to be the number two man on The 700 Club, becoming the only major Black TV preacher in the U.S.

Kinchlow is like an actor turned born-again teacher. His flair for the theatrical included rolling his eyes, swaying back and forth and reaching his arms out for Jesus as he prayed on stage earlier that morning. When he was lecturing (or witnessing, as he prefers to call it) he had the habit of leaving off mid-sentence to let the audience think they had finished his thoughts. Usually the end of each line includes a homily, a bit of American slang, or a quote from the Bible, and his followers had no trouble finishing his sentences.

But during the interview, Kinchlow leaned forward and listened intently to the questions. He finished every sentence himself—I guess because I wouldn't have finished them the way he wanted.

I told him I first heard him speak at Washington for Jesus. What was the upshot of that gathering of the clan?

"Many of the political changes in the U.S. were a result of the gathering together of people at Washington for Jesus. Many of the world's problems that seemed insoluble at that time have receded into the background," he explained confidently. "At that time it looked as though Russia was going to invade Israel at any moment. They invaded Pakistan, Afghanistan and Iran [sic], and the Middle East looked like it was next. Russia was just going to gobble it up. Since that time, a year-and-a-half ago, Russia's had its problems with Cuba—the Cubans are raising Cain—and also in Poland. We also believe the changes in our own government in America are a direct result of a more moral form of government." My mind reeled with this overload of information.

Will the Moral Majority be the leaders of this new government? "Personally, I'm not involved in the Moral Majority, but I'm not criticizing them. What happens is people hear catch prases like Moral Majority and tend to use them like spiritual shorthand. We're talking about people in positions of power in Washington, D.C., with a different view towards what is going on in the country."

But if the born-again Christians get their way, you will have political power and the U.S. will be a Christian as opposed to a multi-religious country, I insisted.

"We're not attempting to take over political power," answered Kinchlow. "We believe every individual should vote his convictions. We are saying that because we are Christians we should not be a persecuted minority. They should not deny us the right to pray; they should not deny us the right to read the Bible. They should not deny us the right to say what we believe, to hold public office or otherwise express our convictions simply because we're born-again Christians. We're not trying to impose a Christian country. We are saying there are certain things that will lead to the downfall of our nation. We are participating in things that will lead to our downfall. It has to do with moral corruption and moral pollution. We are doing things that history has proven to be detrimental to nations. Where families have been done away with; where a strong currency has been done away with; where immorality has been allowed to run rampant. Where divorce has become the law of the land. Where homosexuality is not just allowed, but promoted. These things have caused the downfall of nations throughout history."

American evangelical writer Hal Lindsay, in his runaway bestseller based on Bible prophecy, *The 1980s: Countdown to Armageddon*, writes that the U.S. must arm itself with sophisticated weapons even though they could very well annihilate millions of people. What did Kinchlow think?

Kinchlow looked embarrassed for the first time. "Sure I know Hal Lindsay, but, um, I haven't read *Countdown* yet," he hesitated. "America has a very stable type of government. You are not going to wake up in the morning and read the newspaper to find out that suddenly Washington has been overthrown by dissident religious fanatics, or a left-wing group has suddenly come in. You're just not going to have that."

Two months before the interview I had watched the special

700 Club presentation on TV called "Seven Days of Blaze."
Pat Robertson and Kinchlow used the special to mount a
frontal attack against the American Civil Liberties Union
(ACLU); they even went so far as to say the organization was
founded to foment a communist revolution in the States. I
asked Kinchlow why they condemned a group that defended
human and civil rights in the U.S.?

"First of all, it was not a blanket condemnation of
everyone in the ACLU. There are very dedicated, earnest
attorneys who work with the ACLU who are dedicated to the
principles of liberty. However, if you examine almost every
court case that has to do with the restriction of, the defeat of,
the taking away of, religious rights or religious liberties, you
will find that almost every one of these cases has been
instituted by the ACLU."

But wasn't one of their aims to ensure the separation of
church and state?

"The American people have never said this. There is
nothing in the American government's established system, in
the Constitution, or in the Bill of Rights from the four
founding fathers that supports the concept of the separation
of the church and the state."

So the church and state should be one?

He continued. "We object to that concept. But what the
ACLU is doing is taking away every vestige of every
Christian principle out of the lives of the people. They use the
separation of the church and state as an excuse. All we are
saying is that there is nothing in our Constitution or in our
history that says you cannot belong to the church and be in
government at the same time. What the ACLU is saying is
that if you're going to be a Christian you can't have carols
sung on the White House steps; you can't have prayer
breakfasts; you can't have children observe three minutes of
silence."

Wasn't joining Christianity to centres of power offensive
to people who aren't Christians?

Kinchlow was in his element. "What about the people who

*are?* Don't you believe in God? What we're saying is what's wrong is the fact that people are trying to legislate God *out*. Christian, Jew, Moslem, Buddhist—the ACLU is saying: 'Everybody: you can't have a God.'"

What about the atheists?

"Okay, fine. But you can't forbid God to exist just because you don't believe in Him. They are saying you *cannot* have God. You must have a totally secular society; and if something doesn't have a totally secularized application we can't allow it. That is ridiculous.

"If your son is an atheist, all he has to do is sit there with his eyes closed and say, 'I don't believe in God; I don't believe in God.' That's all. And nobody's gonna force him to believe in God. But by the same token, because he's an atheist, he cannot tell me, 'I refuse to allow you to take three minutes to acknowledge the existence of God.' If your son is a Jew and he's in school and we say, 'We shall observe three minutes of silence in respect to God,' what's wrong with that? They've made it illegal to observe three minutes of silence. That's why they put Jews in the gas ovens in Germany. They said these people refuse to bow down to the state; they are an enemy of the state and they put them in the ovens. That's what they're doing in Russia, that's what they're doing every place where people refuse to acknowledge the supreme power of the state. They isolate them and then they eliminate them."

I thought it wise to change the subject.

On The 700 Club, Pat Robertson talks about your outreach—what is that?

Kinchlow relaxed and smiled. "Well, we have a family network that provides alternative viewing to most of the stuff that is on television. We have the Continental Broadcasting Network that supplies and is producing good, wholesome, family entertainment. Like Another Life, a soap opera; we have a ladies' programme which is called Keeping Time and a morning news show, U.S. A.M.

"We're also involved in the Freedom Council, which is attempting to make people aware of the fact that our religious heritage and liberty is being threatened by people who are trying to wipe out the truth of how America came to be started.

"But the thing I'm most excited about is Operation Blessing, where we try to match the people who have gifts with the people who have needs. Through Operation Blessing we've managed to see hundreds of thousands of dollars put into the hands of people who have no food to eat, no clothes to wear or are being dispossessed because of their rent, mortgage costs or heating oil."

One catch phrase that is used on your TV shows quite often is "secular humanism."

"'Secular humanism,' in effect, says 'Man is God.' Therefore man alone is capable of deciding what is right and what is wrong. There is no higher authority than man and man is not subject to anyone else except himself. That is the basic premise of secular humanism.

"The problem with that is if man is not accountable for his actions, if man is the final authority, then history cannot condemn a man like Adolf Hitler for what he did; it cannot condemn Mao Tse-Tung for what he did. Based on secular humanism, what laws would you use to condemn them? If every man is God, then what Hitler did was justified because Hitler didn't see anything wrong with it."

Isn't there such a thing as valuing human life, even if someone doesn't believe in God?

"Based on what?" Kinchlow asked me. "Do you eat steak? Well, if human life is a product of evolutionary chance, you are no more valuable than a white-faced steer. Why should you be considered more valuable than a white-faced steer? You're not stronger than a lion; you're not faster than a cheetah; you're not more adaptable than a horse. What makes you better?

"You are only better because there is a God who created us in His image, who so loved us that He sent someone to redeem us out of our own mess."

Kinchlow had been a Marine for 13 years. He saw lots of

action and killing in Korea.

"Absolutely right," he replied smugly, "if we did what God said there would be no need for war or for killing. But there are people who will not abide by God's laws. God said if someone does not abide by these laws, if he does not accept My provision for grace, then he must be dealt with according to the laws. And the laws are the foundation for all western society—handed down by Moses on Mount Sinai.

"It is true that when God said don't kill, He also said don't covet. Don't come in and take over your neighbours' land and if you do that you must face the consequences. So we have wars; we have standing armies of righteous men who resist."

But then wasn't the U.S. guilty of entering other peoples' land to covet—like in Vietnam?

Kinchlow solemnly declared, "In every place the U.S. has gone in, it has been in response to aggressors who have come in to take over. This is attributable to the fact that there has always been a God-consciousness of the value of humankind which is directly related to the fact that there is a God."

I decided to change the subject back to religion in the schools.

"As you probably know, public education is a very recent development in America. At one time all education took place in the private schools. When schools became larger, in consultation with families and church, people decided to pool their resources for a central location, pay a teacher who would teach reading, writing and arithmetic predicated on their Christian values. They started every university in America, just about, with the concept of teaching young men about God. I believe Princeton's motto is 'The truth shall make you free'—that is a scriptural quote. Harvard's motto is 'Truth'—God's word is Truth. These universities were established from the concept of teaching young people about God.

"John Dewey, who is considered the father of American education, was an atheist, a secular humanist. He and his group began to take over public education with the express purpose of secularizing it and taking God out of it. The result is the school system that exists in America today, where we have graduate students who cannot read, write or do simple math problems that will allow them to balance a cheque book. We see teachers retiring with battle fatigue and schools where there are assaults and murders."

But aren't all the problems in the schools just reflections of American society's larger problems?

"You know why we have all these problems? Go back to the time the Supreme Court outlawed prayer in the schools and you'll find a gradual increase in violence as society became more secularized. From the point at which they took God out, violence came in."

Is that like saying if you take God out, Satan comes in?

"That's right. If you take away the God consciousness, say from yourself as a Jew, you have a Jew like Karl Marx or like Engels [sic], who were the fathers of communism, and who have enslaved literally millions of people."

I stared.

"When you lose the consciousness of God you've got to replace it with something. And there is nothing that can give value and dignity to humankind except God."

I argued that there are plenty of countries in the world where the Christian notion of God isn't really important to the people—in Russia, in China, in India, in Africa. "Who am I to say that God has to be important to these people?"

"Ma'am," said Kinchlow sternly, "that's easy for you to say because you live under the auspices of a government that has been founded on the bedrock fact of the existence of God. Therefore governments are responsible to God and responsible to their people and the people have rights that cannot be abrogated. Because you live in this country you cannot conceive of living in a country where one man decreed the death of one million people. It doesn't affect you. I am sure you couldn't reasonably argue the defence of more of what Adolf Hitler did during World War II, can you?"

I rushed to answer. "Of course not," I said impatiently. "But I am sure that Hitler called himself a Christian. People all over the world fought against Hitler—Communists, too. Russia lost 20 million people in the war, six million Jews were killed, and tens of thousands of Canadians and Americans lost their lives. Everyone fought because the fascist system of government was extremely detestable."

Kinchlow brightened. "What you are describing is the essence of what communism is today." Oh no. He was starting another round.

"But Hitler wiped out 20 million Communists..."

"The Communists, since they've been in power, have wiped out 100 million people. Mao Tse-Tung in his great leap forward to modernize China killed 25 million of his own people. Germany is divided right down the middle because there is a wall and the people on the communist side—who are just misunderstood people—say that if you try to get across to see your mother or sick brother, we'll blow you up. That's the way it is in Germany and wherever the Communists have taken over. Hey, I'm not a Red-baiter, I'm just saying that wherever you have a system where God is not in power..."

"Satan comes in," I finished his sentence and then realized what I'd done. Kinchlow smiled broadly.

# 6
# Snapped for the Lord

Jean's house was on the edge of Shelburne, a town 100 kilometres northwest of Toronto. Shelburne used to be the hub of fiercely White Anglo-Saxon Protestant Orange country. "The first Black family moved into Orangeville near here seven years ago," Jean told me bluntly. "As Catholics, we were first whispered about, then openly discriminated against when my family moved here ten years ago."

Jean is an attractive, red-headed woman of 23. She was living at home with her parents so she could save enough money from her job at the local K-Mart to go on a trip to Europe and return in time for university next fall.

I stared at her while she was brewing me some tea. "How could you get involved with the born agains, get turned off and quit all before you were out of high school?"

She laughed easily and asked if I'd ever heard of Teen Ranch. "No, why?" I replied.

"Because that's where it all began," Jean said.

Teen Ranch. I remembered I had passed a large wooden sign on a red-brick fence on Highway 10, just south of Orangeville en route to Shelburne.

Jean lit a cigarette and began. "When I'm not stocking shelves at K-Mart, I play amateur ice-hockey on a girl's team in town.

"One summer, when I was 14, a friend on the team told me

about Teen Ranch [in Caledon, Ontario]—a place she went to practise hockey during summer holidays. I convinced my parents I had to go too.

"I should have been suspicious the first day. We rose at 7:00 a.m. In our bunkhouse there were 11 girls and one counsellor. After saying grace and eating breakfast, we loaded all our hockey gear into the bus and set off for the arena in Bolton a few miles away. On the bus we prayed for a safe trip there, and prayed that we'd play good hockey. On our way back, we prayed again for a safe trip and for God to see us through the rest of the day. After lunch there was a Bible Study class we all attended which concentrated on the four gospels and the books of Genesis and Revelation. Time after time the counsellors emphasized that we should each accept Jesus as our personal Saviour. At night, there was always a campfire gathering which featured what amounted to a sermon by the camp director on a Bible passage, and usually testimony by one of the counsellors on how he or she had been a sinner for years before finding Christ and how life had improved since he had accepted the Lord.

"I was sort of suspicious. Though I grew up in a Catholic home, went to a Catholic school and believed in God, I was used to a more formal and less emotional style of religion. But it seemed for that week and a half my whole life was an emotional rollercoaster and I was turned around time after time by both the individual attention I received from my counsellor and the campfire sermons each night.

"After a few days, every girl in my bunkhouse got converted. I was present at 12-year-old Lisa's conversion. Our counsellor, who was probably a university or Bible College student, was discussing Revelation with us when Lisa boldly came forward and insisted she wanted to accept Jesus Christ as her personal Lord and Saviour. We rejoiced at the news.

"After five days at the ranch, it seemed normal to pray for a safe trip to the arena and back again. It took those five days for me to be converted. My counsellor invited me out for a walk and little 'fellowship'—which meant discussing some part of the New Testament.

"We sat by the pond and held hands. She prayed with me to accept Christ. That was my baptism. It was very emotional; we were crying and hugging each other. Good news travelled fast. By the time I got back to the camp, the other counsellors who had been praying for me were congratulating me. I had been on a number of people's prayer lists: finally I was baptized. There was a lot of pressure on me and the other campers to go home and convert friends and classmates. Relatives were targeted, too.

"I remember thinking what sinners my parents and older sister were, and I longed to get back home to start working on their conversions."

A tall vivacious woman with hazel eyes peeked into the room. I asked Jean's mother what Jean was like when she picked her up after the week at the ranch.

"When we went to pick her up, we found a very pale, very hysterical little girl. She wouldn't calm down. We couldn't get much out of her about that week, except that she kept on shrieking she'd become a born-again Christian. I turned to my husband and said, 'What does that mean? Maybe it means that it didn't take the first time.'" Mrs. Evans watched me smile and added, "Neither of us was smiling then—we wondered how long this stage was going to last. After all, most young people go through a stage of rejecting their parents and following their own paths. But this seemed more serious to me. All we could do was weather the storm. But Jean's personality definitely had changed from being a shy, helpful girl to being an overbearing, parrot-like creature. It frightened me."


"Your friend's story is a little hard for me to believe," Mel Stevens, director of Teen Ranch, told me on the phone. "We make no bones about it. This is a Christian camp but we're very low-key here. However we don't compromise the message at all—a personal relationship with Jesus Christ, that's the goal stated on the first page of our brochure."

He's right about that. The glossy eight-page booklet *is* very low-key. Even more low-key is the Hockey Camp brochure, which merely states, "Teen Ranch was established in 1967 as a registered, charitable, non-sectarian, Christian organization. The philosophy of the camp is to provide quality personnel, programs and facilities while encouraging the complete development of young people in physical, spiritual, intellectual and social areas of their lives."

But what about Jean's parents' complaints?

"Well," argued Stevens, "when kids come here and become born again and go home and tell their folks, it can be a threat to a parent. It's like saying to the parent: 'You haven't brought me up right,' and no one wants to hear that."

Doesn't the hothouse atmosphere pressure kids to convert?

"We're not trying to convert kids to Christianity," Stevens replied. "It's just that we've found Christianity to be a viable force in modern life. We don't apply pressure to try to get a convert. But many young people have had their lives turned around by a born-again experience."

Mel Stevens and his wife Janet started the camp in 1967 by themselves, "with the help of a lot of kind people," Stevens acknowledges. The ranch has a staff of over 40 in the summers and a dozen in the wintertime but the counsellors receive no pay. Most of them are teachers and university students who volunteer time to help younger people during their vacations.

Are there any Bible school students? "No," Stevens told me, "I don't have anything against Bible school students but often they get to feel too much like experts and just end up spouting Scripture. Our philosophy is that if we're living our lives in a manner which glorifies God, more will be caught than taught." He chuckled. In addition to the hockey camp during the summer months, Teen Ranch offers Indian Camp. "The kids live in Blackfoot Indian teepees and do Indian crafts," he explained. A Riding Camp, Tennis Camp, Rugger Camp, Hockey Camp and "Wham Week" are also offered.

All the cabins on the rolling 150-acre ranch are fully winterized to house the hockey and football teams which practise there on weekends and over the winter.

Stevens, who is also chaplain to the Toronto Argonauts football team, explained the ranch's programme. "We have a preventative programme here. We attract young people from all walks of life and even kids from Germany, Sweden and England. We tell them that when their lives are centred on Jesus Christ they don't need to turn to drugs or alcohol.

"For every story you tell me like that girl's, there are stories like this," he stressed. "We had a 12-year-old boy come to Hockey Camp about ten years ago. His mother was a Christian, but his father, an Air Canada pilot, was dead set against religion. The boy asked Jesus Christ to forgive his sins and come into his life. Now, at 22, the boy is still a Christian and in third-year university. I suggested that his mother go to a local Bible Study class for ladies, which she did. Finally the father even converted. The older daughter went to Bible school in Texas. Then the father quit his pilot's job and the whole family, except the son, packed up and went into missionary work in Manitoba."

For the first time, Stevens seemed miffed.

"Yes, your girl's story is amazing to me. It's strange. Obviously she didn't do any growing as a Christian while she was at camp."

I asked Jean what happened after Teen Ranch.

"I became part of an organization called Campus Life. In the fall, I went to the local secondary school instead of commuting some distance, as I had, to the private Catholic high school. For the first time I was thrown into an environment that was co-educational, non-denominational and riddled with dope, uppers, downers and booze. At my other school I had indulged in soft drugs, but at the public high school it seemed like open season.

"I was a born-again Christian now. No drinking, no drug taking, just praying and reading the Bible. During the fall I went out with Campus Life people regularly. When I'd go out for coffee or tea with a born-again friend, we'd sit in a restaurant holding each other's hands tightly, praying aloud. Wednesday night was Bible Study night; I'd go to a friend's house and tune into all the meanings and prescribed interpretations of sections of the Bible. The born agains were very big on the four Gospels and Revelation. To them, the rest of the Bible hardly existed.

"Often, after the Bible Study sessions, there would be a discussion, usually on morality. The people in the fellowship didn't even have time to read the newspaper, let alone discuss current events. I became more and more out of touch with what was happening in the world. My world was praying, repenting and witnessing.

"I remember one discussion we had about the evils of abortion. The Campus Lifers were dead set against abortion. 'Abortion under no circumstances' was their motto. I asked, 'Does that mean if a 12-year-old girl gets raped in a vicious attack she should be made to have the baby?' Yes, they told me, adoption was always available after the baby is born."

Jean paused to pour more tea and let her cat out on the window ledge. "Another lecture I remember quite well revolved around Margaret Trudeau. Yes," she smiled and shook her head, "Margaret Trudeau. The Campus Life leader explained that it was going against God for her to have left her family. It was immoral. I didn't see it that way. After all, how many men had left their wives and children before becoming born-again? They weren't put down. There seemed to be a double standard for men and women I wasn't happy about.

"One thing I resent to this day is the role of the school board in promoting Campus Life. About three times a year, throughout my high school years, an assembly was called in the cafeteria. Once all the students filed in and sat down, a band of clean-cut young guys, along with their scrubbed roadies, came in, set up the stage and started to play popular tunes like "You Light Up My Life." Usually the group was introduced by one of the businessmen in the community whom everyone knew—often he was a member of some businessmen's group. After the introduction, the band played a medley of popular, upbeat tunes and toned-down gospel music for over an hour. There was not a mention of religion at all. After the show, we were reminded that the band would be playing again Wednesday night for a nominal fee at the school, and we were invited to come out to hear the entertainment and have a good time.

"Campus Life had no trouble invading the school, and this same school board actually banned Margaret Laurence's *The Diviners* from English courses and wouldn't let Michael Ondaatje's *The Collected Works of Billy the Kid* sit on the library shelf at the school."

The secretary put me right through to the director of the Dufferin Board of Education. "Well, I've only been the director for a year and a half," Stan Robinson explained to me pleasantly.

What about book bannings? "Yes, I seem to remember something like that happening some years ago. No, I don't think any books are banned now. While *The Diviners* is not on the curriculum, it is available in the school libraries."

Have any parents complained about Campus Life operating within the high schools? Mr. Robinson thought for a moment. "No, I haven't received any complaints. Normally the staff at the schools are the first to object to a new programme, but in this case everyone at the schools feels the Campus Life representatives are sincere and helpful people. They bring moral and ethical values to our students and assist our guidance departments in helping students who have personal problems. I don't see why anyone would be against them." But Robinson was a more active participant than he let on, I discovered.

Paul Robertson, a 32-year-old former marketing teacher from Belleville, was the regional director for Campus Life in Dufferin County, visiting the Shelburne High School on Tuesdays and Thursdays and the Orangeville High School Mondays, Wednesdays and Fridays.

"I have a good working relationship with most of the teachers in both schools," he told me in a phone interview. "The principals and the director of education are behind me. Every two months, I nip into Mr. Robinson's office and discuss programmes I am working on, and *he'll pass along any names of students who might need my help.* You see, I am a missionary. The high school scene is no different from deepest, darkest Africa and I am on the front line."

I asked him if he knew that *The Diviners* had been banned several years ago. He admitted he never heard of the book so I told him it was about a young woman from rural Manitoba who moves to Toronto, and marries, leaves her husband for an extra-marital relationship with an Indian from a northern settlement. Before I could finish, he asked me if I would want my kids to read it.

"Yes," I replied without hesitation.

"Well, I wouldn't want my kids to read it. It sounds like garbage to me."

When I asked Robertson about the message behind the school assemblies, he explained readily. "When we go into a school, we make no bones about being Christians. Bible thumping doesn't work with the kids or with the staff. Since the school assemblies are compulsory for students, we are careful about what we say to them. For instance, a year ago, Ron Moore from Michigan came up and sang secular songs and rattled off a few humorous stories. He didn't preach any message; the message was in the music. That evening we invited the kids back to hear more gospel music with a light message."

"Hundreds of kids showed up to the Wednesday night parties," Jean told me. "Posters around the school publicized a get-together for laughs and a good time at Campus Life. No one was really suspicious of them. Admission was anywhere from 75 cents to $2.50: there was no collection. There was no dancing; students sat on chairs and listened to speakers who were witnessing their faith and the well-turned out backup band whose managers wore three-piece suits.

"There was no overt religious proselytizing during the evenings. Delivery of jokes and patter between the songs was smooth.

"Another event held at the school each year was the "Gym Riot." Campus Life organized the Gym Riot as a games night for students—silly games like tying six people together to race to beat the clock—that sort of thing. They brought Athletes in Action to those Gym Riots. I am interested in sports and I got to meet people like Toronto Argonaut football players Peter Muller, Zenon Andruzyshyn, and Chuck Ealey and hockey coaches Doug Jarvis and Ron Ellis. Once I even got to play football with Chuck Ealey at Teen Ranch. Many students besides me were impressed meeting the athletes. More so when each one of them, as if on cue, explained, 'This is how I found the Lord.' This witnessing, as we called it, would pique the students' interest in Campus Life.

"Campus Life never seemed to be short of funds. They charged a nominal fee for every event but they never took collections. Once they sent letters to all the parents of the students involved and asked them to attend an information meeting. My mother went, but walked out when she discovered all they wanted was money.

"In fact, my parents were deliberately excluded from any discussion or plans. At Teen Ranch we were told that after we accepted Jesus as Lord, people were going to persecute us—especially our parents. The only easy way to guard against their Satanic influence was to narrow our lives to born-again activities like reading the religious books that were passed around the group: *Teenagers' Guide to Christian Living* or books by C. S. Lewis. We weren't supposed to go to parties, or to swear, and our only friends came to be people who believed in the Bible as we did. We were never encouraged to be 'stewards' or to work at helping our fellow man though we were born again. To me now, this seems rather un-Christian; at the time we were told the only important things we could do were repent our past and witness and give testimony to classmates or relatives."

What was Jean's testimony?

Jean laughed. "My testimony went something like this: 'I used to be a sinner. As a young teenager I was into drugs and alcohol. I no longer take those things and that is because I am in this world but I am not of this world—I am here for a short time only. Now I have a personal relationship with Jesus Christ and there is no emptiness in my life. I know where I'm headed.'

"My testimony seemed thin even to me. How could I have been such a terrible sinner for the first 14 years of my life? How could everything of the world be the work of the Devil? If God loves people and is a forgiving God, why did He let the Holocaust happen, I asked? Because the Devil has power and control over the world, any wrongdoings by man are under the eye of Satan, I was told. The more I questioned, the more I was told the Devil made me doubt!

"Another point I never quite understood was the born again's insistence that the New Testament was the literal word of God—even though it was translated from Greek to Hebrew to English and had been handed down through the centuries. Of course, they told me, we don't quite believe everything in the Old Testament, and many of the stories like Jonah and the Whale they consider parables. Once I asked how Noah could possibly have fit all those animals on one ark? My friends told me the Old Testament was often just parables. Then I asked why, if God wrote the whole New Testament beginning to end, had He written the four gospels under different names? 'Oh,' I was told, 'That is because it would be fishy to people if all four gospels were exactly the same.'

"I was skeptical. How could the Campus Life people say exactly what the Bible meant and give the only true interpretation?"

Paul Robertson listened to me tell him about Jean's experience. "Look, my philosophy is that we present kids with new information and they can take it from there. Either you're part of the Kingdom of God or you're not. I only wish people in the churches would come and spend a day with me, talking to the students. It would give them a little dose of reality therapy."

Campus Life is a division of Youth For Christ, a U.S.-based organization with branches in 57 countries worldwide. Campus Life started in 1952 with evangelist Billy Graham as its first full-time worldwide organizer. "We're in 35 centres across Canada, from Montreal to Victoria," Robertson told me. "We have requests from places like Ottawa we can't even fill yet. It is the local people who want to see a centre start. We have groups in eight or ten schools in Etobicoke [a Toronto suburb] where we have 14 full-time Campus Life staffers. We have groups in Scarborough and in Mississauga—but none in Toronto."

What is reality therapy?

"In the course of one day, I talk to high school kids who have attempted suicide, who are pregnant, who are caught up in drugs. I spend the time to listen to them. I am supportive to them. If it's a non-Christian kid, I'll pray for him and he won't know it. I have a lady who is in the United Church in town who is heading up a prayer chain. So far we've got 45 people on the chain who are willing to listen to young people who phone them."

Doesn't he get hostile comments from parents or members of the staff at the schools? "Not really," Robertson says.

"Most of the parents' concerns are that their kids don't get involved in any cult. It doesn't seem reasonable to me for them to object to their kids becoming Christians. There is nothing to join, no membership dues. It is true that cults believe that God is love, but they don't believe that the Bible is the truth."

Who pays Robertson? "I raise my own salary," he boasted. "I operate on faith. Parents give money to the ministry; I get no support from the local churches. I figure if God created the universe, He can scrape up enough money to get me by," Robertson laughed. "In 18 months on the job, I've missed one pay cheque and that was because of the mail strike!"

But what about people who think it is wrong to preach Christianity in a public school system which is not supposed to cater to any one religious group?

"You are telling me that religion has no place in the schools, but secular humanism does! You see, by not pushing a religion, you're really having a religion and that is secular humanism. The Ontario Ministry of Education says that one and a half hours a week should be devoted to Judeo-Christian studies. Now this is ignored by many school boards. You can sit in a classroom and hear a teacher preach his own beliefs to students any day. But we get pot shots because we believe in Jesus Christ."

Jean continued her story.

"The school year ended and it was summer holidays again. There was a tent meeting in Orangeville to which an American evangelist was brought up from the States," Jean said. "The night I went I noticed a number of respectable, leading citizens of the town were there. At the door were two huge men who looked more like bouncers at a bar than ticket-takers. There was a choir, organ music, gospel songs and a big banner behind the stage which read 'Jesus Saves.' The pastor, all dressed in white, drifted up to the microphone.

"He started out by telling the story of Jesus and Barrabas on the cross. I remember him shouting, 'You can live your life according to Jesus or Barrabas.' Then he launched into a story of a man in a hospital bed whose family had accepted Christ but he had not. He was close to death and finally, answering his family's prayers, accepted the Lord. He was saved and eventually recovered. Before the story was finished, the crowd roared out 'Amen—Hallelujah!' People threw up their hands and started swaying, crying and screaming.

"All of a sudden it hit me. The whole meeting didn't make any sense. What did the Bible story have to do with the man in the hospital? The emotion and panic in the audience shattered my belief. I got scared; doubts were crossing my mind. The two big guys at the door, would they let me out? I started to run, through the crowd, past the hulks at the door and outside. I couldn't stop running until I got back into town.

"That night was the turning point for me. It made me take a look at what these people were saying. I began to accept that it was a natural process to have questions and not to accept things blindly. The people at that Tent Meeting were so hysterical they couldn't think anymore and that is the most dangerous aspect of the born-again movement."

As I looked out the window I noticed the street lights were on. The sky was a deep indigo blue, and the horizon was a slash of red. "What finally happened?"

"I grew more and more distant from the group. They called me and were solicitous—what was making me fall away from the group? Maybe I needed some extra prayer or I needed to repent a bit more, they gently suggested. Could we meet for coffee? But I was on the road to becoming too worldly; I realized I was a humanist—a no-no for the born agains because that meant getting away from God.

"I began to read about Marxist theory and tried to talk to my friends in Campus Life but they were rabidly anti-communist, because they insisted socialism was anti-God. The sole topic of conversation with them was what to pray about. They had tunnel vision. I realized I was a naturally curious, even skeptical person. I wanted to know what was behind things. I started seeing my Christian friends less and less. They started to lose interest in me; in fact most of them have even stopped praying for me. And after two years, it's no wonder," Jean laughed.

What worries you the most about the born-again Christian movement?

"On a personal level, I guess I'm bitter because I was sucked in. I feel I lost a couple of valuable years of my life and I feel let down. My chief concern is that they seem to get people at a young and vulnerable age, when kids are testing the running ground. By a vulnerable age, I mean that those teen years are a time when kids need their parents for love and guidance but on the other hand need some independence and tend to reject their parents' authority. Wherever Campus Life speaks, I wish I could get onto the stage and tell the students what they are all about."

Were there any positive aspects to your born-again experience?

"In a way, the experience helped me. It gave me peace of mind for a while during a time of my life that was fraught with dissatisfaction and anger. I had something to believe in. But their intolerance of any other religion and any other viewpoint is frightening and it bothers me that they are in the schools. That type of religion stunts people's growth spiritually and intellectually. I was cut off from world literature, movies, theatre and politics—that can be dangerous."

Jean opened the window and reached out for her cat who had been staring in at us from the ledge. "I guess what those two years mainly did was give me a different perspective on life. Now I am pretty sure I could start my own religion. I know all the tricks of the trade. The first thing I'd do is zoom in on kids aged 12 to 15. I'd start off being chummy-chummy with them. I'd use professional athletes and clean-cut adults to be role-models for them. The brainwashing would be subtle and smooth. For some students, that kind of treatment and nurturing might last much longer than it did in my case. And that is what we have to guard against."

---
# 7
# Fellowship Begins at Home

*I've just come to praise the Lord,*
*I've just come to praise the Lor-r-rd,*
*I've just come to praise his holiness,*
*I've just come to praise the Lord.*


Susie's voice rang out clear and gutsy as it had on the 12-hour bus ride to the Washington for Jesus rally. Now the bus ride and gathering of the born-again clan were more than a year behind us and she was leading a hymn-sing at a prayer fellowship meeting in her own living room in Mississauga, near Toronto. At the end of one song, she started another, one I was familiar with because I'd heard it many times on TV's 100 Huntley Street.


*Hallelujah, Praise the Lord,*
*Hallelujah, sing with joy,*
*Hallelujah the bells are going to ring,*
*Just open up your heart and sing,*
*Hal-lay-lu-yah!*

Then she launched into a series of gospel tunes and upbeat hymns that she took from *The Catacombs Song Book* which was lying on the coffee table in front of her; her husband Emilio accompanied her on his guitar.

After the Washington trip, Susie had issued me a standing invitation to join her fellowship for a Sunday service, and I was taking her up on it. As I looked around the room, the faces were smiling and the hands were clapping in time to the music.

The fellowship is small and informal, comprising a few families living near each other in an older Mississauga neighbourhood. As Tim, a former congregant at a fair-sized Baptist church, told me before leaving to work on a farm in New Brunswick run by a few Christian sisters: "We don't need a big building with a leader. We each have a personal relationship with Jesus Christ, and we don't feel we have to be part of a church to be Christians."

Besides their Sunday morning meeting, the men in the group get together for a breakfast fellowship before work at least once a week, while the "girls" have coffee parties a couple of times a week. One night a week everybody in the group gathers for Bible Study. They also speak to each other on the telephone every day. Susie explains: "We live close to each other and help each other. Churches don't do that nowadays. They don't seem to serve their members the way we do. We aren't just Sunday Christians."

Susie, who comes from Buffalo, New York, was born an Episcopalian; and since her conversion has developed great philosophical differences with her parents.

"My parents still go to church on Sundays but like many people who call themselves Christians, they don't believe in miracles anymore and in God's supernatural power at all. I can't get them to think that today God acts the way He did in the New Testament. My parents don't believe that God has the power He did to heal and raise people from the dead. They believe that today science and technology explain a lot of the miracles that took place in the Bible. That's why they think they only need to go to church on Sundays. They put their belief in science and medicine instead of in God."

The houses on Susie's street were more like cottages than the suburban bungalows I'd expected to see in Mississauga. She lived in an old part of town near Lake Ontario. Her one-and-a-half-storey house was set back from the road, with a white picket fence around the front yard. As I walked up the steps I got the feeling she described—a small-town feeling—reinforced by gospel singing from the living room as I stood on the porch.

Susie greeted me warmly. She wore a tweed skirt and a soft wool sweater, and her hair was elegantly styled. Despite the fact that she had twins ten months old, she was a walking model of born-again author Marabel Morgan's *Total Woman*. Pretty, feminine and devoted to her God and her family.

As I walked into her modest but spotless living room, the twins were sitting on the laps of the two other woman members. Ellen, about 18, was thin and nervous-looking. She sat on the couch beside the leader of the group, Al, a blond-bearded man of about 30, who shook my hand as I sat down.

Al's wife, Holly, seven months pregnant, sat wrapped in a shawl serenely rocking in a rocking chair by the window. Emilio, Susie's husband, was accompanying the singers on his guitar.

After the hymns and gospel songs were over the praying began. Susie closed her eyes tightly. "Lord, I thank you for bringing Judy to this service. I hope she will...," she hesitated, "feel free to participate."

"Amen," everyone else murmured.

"Lord," Holly's face was troubled. "Please help Joan, one of us who is in hospital facing a serious operation. I pray she recovers and that You will give her the strength to carry on."

A few seconds of silence and "Amens."

More silence, while members prayed to themselves and the babies babbled.

After a few minutes, Al pointed to a portable tape recorder on the coffee table. He explained that the tape was a recording he had made when Elisabeth Elliot, an American evangelist and missionary, had spoken in Toronto six months before. Her sermon was called "The Shaping of Christian Character."

Elliot's voice was frosty as it crackled from the small speakers in the portable cassette tape recorder. "Who are the people who have most influenced my life?" she asked. "Well, they are not my peers, many of whom have turned out to be middle-aged hippies!" Her audience laughed their approval. "The people who influenced me the most were the people who believed in God. I thank God I grew up in a Christian home. A Christian home meant discipline. A word you don't hear today very often." A pause and some clapping from her listeners.

"We Christians have to put ourselves under obedience to God. 'If it feels good, do it' is subliminally taught by advertising in our society, but it is certainly not taught in the Bible.

"My father used to wake up every day at 4:30 or 5:00 a.m. He didn't wake up then because he wanted to or because he loved to get up early. He woke up at that time because it was the only time of the day when he could get free time to pray and to lead the family in devotions. The six of us youngsters also had discipline in our lives. Every morning, our ritual began with us working through the hymn book, reading part of the Bible, saying our morning prayers and ending with Dad reading the Lord's Prayer." Some surprised chatter in the audience.

"Only after we finished were we allowed to go to breakfast which my mother served at 7:10 sharp. There was no skipping the family devotions in our house. Every day the routine was the same, even on holidays away camping. That routine took sacrifice, self-discipline and plain old-fashioned guts on the part of my father. He didn't enjoy getting up so early; he didn't enjoy leaving the house to catch the commuter train every morning at 7:50, but these were the things he had to do.

"And that was far from the end of our Christian upbringing. Every day we worked through the hymn book twice. If we slacked off or were late, my mother would just have to look at the switch above the doorway. That look alone would get us back to devotions or to jobs around the house.

People nowadays tell me that was fine for people in those days, but today, life is so complicated that kind of routine will never work. Well, I have news for those people. Life was just as tough, just as complicated when I was young as it is today. The ingredient that is missing is self-discipline. If you watch television, or go out till all hours in the morning or live a me-first life, how do you expect your children to grow up and become Christians?"


"You know," said Al after the sermon ended, "the only thing most of us lack in our lives, that Elisabeth Elliot has, is absolute faith.

"You know she was a linguist and a missionary to a tribe of people in Ecuador for quite a while. She was moved to translate the Bible into their language but the problem was that their language was not a written one. So she had to find a person who knew the tribe's language and knew Spanish, who would help her translate the Bible. Well, she found a person who had grown up in the village, gone away to a big city in South America and returned. He was also a Christian and willing to teach her the tribe's language and together they wrote the language for the first time. God had delivered that man to her.

"According to Elisabeth Elliot, one day there was some sort of fight in the village and by the time she knew what was happening, the man had been killed.

"Now a person of less faith would have given up. She

would have said, 'This proves there is no God because why would an understanding God destroy a person so necessary to help carry on missionary work?'"

The people in the room sat straighter to hear Al's interpretation of Elliot's story.

"But she knew in her heart that God has His reasons for doing what He does," Al thundered.

"That is what self-discipline and faith are all about. There is no such thing as half-belief in God. *My* faith rests totally in God."

"Amen," cried the other three together. "Praise the Lord."

A few minutes of silence went by. Suddenly Al asked if anyone had anything they wanted to discuss. Susie bowed her head. "Lord, please give me the patience I need to handle the children better."

Emilio put down the guitar, stretched up his hands and closed his eyes, "Lord, please help me to be compassionate to the patients I meet at work in the hospital.

Holly said, "I just want to be a good caring mother, Lord."

Ellen was quiet. Al looked at me, but I smiled no thanks.

He picked up the wine glass from the tray in front of him, tore off a piece of bread from a plate and handed them to Ellen. He told her that the wine and bread represented the blood and body of Jesus who died for their sins. She took a sip, ate the crust and passed on the glass and another crust to Holly. The communion went around the room and ended with Al. Al announced that the services were over. It was time for lunch.

"Elisabeth Elliot raised a good point on that tape," Emilio explained. "As a Christian you have to have the faith in your heart that you are right. That's the belief that she's talking about. Either you believe *every* word that's written in the Bible was divinely inspired by God or you don't believe in any of it."

"Well," I interjected, "There are some things people believe in the Bible and other things they don't. For instance, some people believe there was once a man named Abraham who had a wife named Sarah who couldn't have a child. But those people don't necessarily believe the earth was created in six days."

Holly spoke up. "I find that amazing; then why believe at all? That sounds like a Christian who's allowed doubt and disbelief to take over."

I replied, "No, that's a person who might be part of your Judeo-Christian heritage who believes that certain men existed in the past but that the earth couldn't have been created in six days."

"The real stumbling block for Man according to Scripture is that God chose to come down to this earth which He created and cloak His spirit with flesh and live amongst us. Then He died and was raised up on the third day. It is foolish to deny that," Emilio said. "If a person can't accept that the Lord created the earth in six days, how can he accept that God came to earth as a person? That is more foolish than to believe the world was created in six days. But that is the whole crux of a Christian's life!"

Al pointed to the twin on his lap. "When I see what a miracle life is, how little Ben over here is created from a cell that divides and divides, it boggles my mind that people can believe we are descended from an amoeba in the sea, and that we went from being apes to being men. That staggers me. How can a person believe that? All I can do is believe in Scripture. 'These things will be held from them...for the Lord blinds the eyes of the wise.'"

---
## 8
# The Other Bestseller List

While Canadian secular publishers are scrimping and scraping through hard times, borrowing money at high interest rates, suffering soaring production costs and laying off employees, some religious publishers and their Canadian distributors are taking on a whole new lease on life.

Parallelling the explosion in evangelical radio and TV broadcasting in the 1970s, religious publishing has taken on a whole new image. While Bibles and tracts are still the bestsellers and while the "mainline publishers" (Bantam, Collins, Nelson, Doubleday, Harper and Row) are still the biggest names, they are being challenged by a new crop of publishers, authors and products. Books on family problems, self-awareness, self-help (even money management), prophecy, and Christian novels with biblical themes, are published by companies like Word, Inc., of Waco, Texas (owned by ABC), which now publishes Billy Graham, Zondervan Corp. of Grand Rapids, Michigan (the largest with 1980 sales of $55 million), Chosen Books and Fleming H. Revell Co., which bought paperback rights to Colson's books.

With the new companies and new authors have come all the trappings of secular publishing: agents, big advances, and fierce bidding on subsidiary rights.

"In the 48 years our family has been in this business, we've never seen a downturn," boasts Keith Cheshire, vice-president of R. G. Mitchell Family Books of Toronto, the largest Canadian distributor of U.S. evangelical publishers. "That's not to say we're not aware of what's going on in the economy and keeping an eye on it. We stock 11,000 items and of course it is more difficult to collect money from some bookstores. But our sales were up 40 per cent in July of 1982, over July of 1981."

Religious publishing is the quiet giant. David Duncan, marketing manager of R.G. Mitchell explains, "I was in the secular book trade for 18 years. I came into this business because religious book publishing is booming. It is ahead in technology, more professional, better organized, and more systematized than the secular publishers."

For years the *New York Times* and other North American dailies have ignored the success of the evangelical book market. For instance, the number-one bestseller of 1976 was not Woodward and Bernstein's *The Final Days* as was reported; it was Billy Graham's *Angels*. Graham is still on the top of the religious publishing heap. In 1977 *How to be Born Again*, with an 800,000-copy hardcover first printing (said to be the largest ever), sold more than a million copies. Likewise in 1975, it was not really *Looking for Mr. Goodbar*, but Marabel Morgan's *Total Woman* that topped the lists.

Unlike most bestsellers such as *Princess Daisy* or *Joshua Then and Now*, which are known by an audience far wider their their readership, evangelical bestsellers are only now becoming known to the wider general public.

Non-religious bestsellers traditionally get reviewed in a wide variety of magazines and newspapers; their authors are interviewed on prime-time talk shows; movies and television specials are made about them. Recently religious publishers have been aggressively seeking a share of their space and air time.

But the evangelical book publishers have been even more aggressive than "mainline publishers" in seeking new ways of publicizing and selling their books—which are going like hotcakes.

*The Picture Bible* is a three-volume paperback set of Bible stories in a colour comic-book format—complete with the text in balloons over the characters' heads. It was advertised on television, first by the parent American publisher, then shipped to its subsidiary in Canada. "It was only a 30-second ad, like K-Tel records," explained John Booker, sales manager of David C. Cook Publishing Canada Ltd., "but it ran for a year. In the U.S. we sold nearly a million copies at $12.95. Here in Canada we sold between 25,000 and 30,000 for the slightly higher price of $14.95. Viewers could pay by charge card or C.O.D. We also found it generated a lot of interest in bookstore sales."

He found the comic-book format did upset a few people in the church. "Our biggest criticism came from hard-core conservative Christians who didn't like the way it portrayed people in the Bible. In fact, it's sort of like those Classic comic books—popular when I was a kid. Though *The Picture Bible* is unique, we tried to give the book some degree of dignity. And I think we succeeded.

"Don't think *The Picture Bible* is only for kids. Half the sales are to adults—particularly those at the low end of the literacy scale, like some people in prisons. In Edmonton, *The Picture Bible* was given to every new family of Vietnamese 'Boat People' one church adopted. Soon they'll graduate to one of the myriad of more sophisticated texts."

Television has paid off in a big way for born-again prophet and writer Hal Lindsey. Direct TV sales catapulted his latest evangelical book into a bestseller. His first book, *The Late Great Planet Earth*, first published in 1970 by Bantam Books, has over 15 million copies in print and until recently had sold a steady 5000 books every six months in Canada alone. *The Late Great Planet Earth* claims that recent happenings—from natural catastrophes to the threat of nuclear holocaust—were foreseen by prophets from Moses to Jesus "as being key signals for the coming of an Antichrist."

Lindsay's prophecy for the 1980s shows signs of even

bigger sales—making use of marketing techniques that are relatively new to publishing. For *The 1980s: Countdown to Armageddon*, Lindsey filmed a 60-second commercial that was featured on independent American television stations, selling directly to viewers rather than going through a publisher and bookstores. It is estimated that Lindsey sold over 130,000 hardcover books through this promotion in the first four months. *Countdown to Armageddon* has sold so well because many fundamentalists believe that we are entering the start of the "end of times." Lindsey warns, "When Russia invaded Afghanistan, it took its first step into Ezekiel 38." The book also supports Israel unquestioningly, and explains that the rebirth of Israel as a nation is a welcome sign that the end of the world will come soon.

Though Bible prophecy sells well, so does personal triumph over tragedy. The Joni books are a case in point. Joni Eareckson's autobiography, *Joni*, and its sequel, *One Step Further*, are personal experience stories about "a young quadriplegic's struggle to accept and adjust to her handicap and find meaning in life." In addition to being a bestselling author, Joni, aged 34 and confined to a wheelchair, continues to paint intricate and beautiful watercolour sketches, line drawings of wildlife, and pastoral scenes, all with a paintbrush between her teeth. She has founded her own Christian fellowship in California called "Joni and Friends" and supports the fellowship and herself through the sales of her artwork and proceeds from the sales of both her books. She makes frequent television appearances on the evangelical talk-show circuit and has been a guest on Canada's 100 Huntley Street.

All of this is amazing, considering the severity of her disability. But her faith is unshakable. Both her books have sold tens of thousands of copies in Canada. In the first six months of 1980, *Joni* sold 10,300 copies. Now a feature-length movie, with Joni playing herself, it premiered in western Canada. R. G. Mitchell Family Books (the Canadian distributor for Zondervan), expects interest from the film, coupled with a mass-market paperback edition of *One Step Further*, will set new sales records.

"Our biggest seller is still the Bible," says Cheshire. "The first six months of 1982, we sold 32,000 of the New International Version alone. In total during that time, we sold 60,000 Bibles."

And he's not the only one. David Falle, president of Lawson Falle Ltd. of Cambridge, Ontario, distributes the Nelson line of Bibles. "We sell an average of 25,000 copies a year of the King James Version. The New American Standard Translation, which costs anywhere from $6.50 to $75.00, sells 14-15,000 each year. W. H. Smith, Coles, Classic's, Eaton's, and Simpson's are constantly replenishing their stocks of Bibles."

Jack Cole, former president of Coles bookstores, agrees. "We stock Bibles and hymnals but not much else in terms of religious books here. But religious books are an absolute ingredient to the success of our 23 stores in the southern U.S. Bible Belt."

Religious bookstores have sprung up all across Canada as well. In 1970, at the first Christian Booksellers Association convention, which was held in Guelph, Ontario, there were 47 Christian booksellers registered to view seven book exhibits. Twelve years later, at their convention in Hamilton, Ontario, 275 member bookstores registered, and over 525 stores were represented. Glen Cameron, executive director of the Christian Booksellers Association in Canada, is certain recent developments in Christian publishing "bring much pleasure to our Lord. . . . As God's fellow workers, the onus is on us to share in a ministry of mutual encouragement."

To what does he attribute the success of the evangelical publishers? "In times of trouble, people turn to inspirational books. Many stores are still showing growth and optimism."

Murray Tindale, general manager of E. P. Bookshops, which has four locations in the Toronto area, told me his sales this year are equal to last year or better. "I'll tell you a little secret," he said over the phone. "I have a brother-in-law who is a staff superintendent for the Metropolitan Police. He tells me, 'Murray, I don't know how anyone can live in our society without God.' And our sales bear that out. Do you know what people are buying these days? The experimental type of books have had their day. People are reading more inspirational books and Christian literature.

"People are in trouble and are looking to improve their spiritual condition. They begin to see the errors in the way they've lived and are looking for a way out. That solution isn't booze and drugs."

What's selling? "Well the new King James Version of the Bible, the fifth revision came out recently," said Mr. Tindale. "We bought 150 clothbound editions and sold them at $14.95. We also brought out 50 in leather at $32.95. We sold out of all of those in three weeks. That Bible is moving and is a good volume item."

Another successful store is Edmonton's Canadian Bible Society Bookstore. Bookstore manager Lana Bills curtly says their figures are "classified," but readily admits they have the largest volume of sales for any Christian retail store in Canada. They are the charter winner of the CBA's Bookstore of the Year Award.

"Well, they can't give it to us *every* year," she sniffs, "even though we continue to sell the most." What sells?

"People are looking for self-improvement and personal discipline books," says Bills, "how to get more out of life, how to stop becoming a zombie in our society. Often people come in to pick up classics, like the Bible, or they come out of curiosity."

But there didn't seem to be many people there who were "just plain curious." The day I wandered into the store in Edmonton, most were there for a definite reason. A couple of people to whom I spoke were Sunday school teachers; the person ahead of me at the cash register was a Full Gospel Businessman. The atmosphere was relaxing and quiet. Aquamarine carpets muffled the sound of voices and the shuffle of crepe-soled clerks who were forever straightening

*Top left*: A wall of novelties—bumper stickers at The Christian Booksellers Convention held in Toronto. *Top right*: The Adam and Eve Family Tree—a poster-size history of the universe, from Creation to the present. *Below*: Mainroads Production (part of the 100 Huntley Street Ministry) features records by born-again performers.

*Top*: The Anglican Book Centre display. *Below*: Positive Thoughts—wall plaques with Bible messages.

A collection of Spire Christian Comics, published by the Fleming H. Revell Company of New Jersey. Revell is one of the most respected Christian publishers.

A page from *Hansi*, one of the Spire Christian Comics series.

book displays and lining up knick-knacks on shelves. A homogenized but respectably upbeat sound wafted from the speakers at a barely noticeable level. "It was probably the Terry Talbots or the Bob Bennetts. People today want records with meaty, Christian lyrics," I was told by Bills.

The store sells records, priced competitively with secular music at $9.95 and up, as well as a few book marks, pens and pocket crosses. The store services over 250 cash customers each day, and over 300 Sunday schools across Alberta. All of the 15 employees have had "a personal experience with Jesus Christ," says Bills. "We did hire people without that kind of background, but they just weren't comfortable here."

Most of the stock is imported from the U.S. evangelical publishers such as Zondervan, Tyndale House and Moody Press. With the imports come a rise in book prices on this side of the border. "We have found no consumer resistance to the 25 cent markup which covers freight and exchange," Bills told me. "We have answers and hope for people in crisis. I guess you could say this is one type of business that isn't suffering right now."

Mervyn McKinney, manager of the main E. P. (Evangelical Publishers) Bookshop in Toronto bemoans the fact that there are so few Canadian Christian books. "It's really too bad, but 90 percent of our material is from the U.S. One Canadian supplier may represent a dozen U.S. publishers. In our shop we feature Canadian authors. But it is hard for them to get published because they are unknown south of the border." E. P. Bookshop features a rack of Canadian-authored evangelical books near the front of the store.

A Canadian-authored blockbuster is *A Shepherd Looks at Psalm 23* by Phillip Keller. It is number seven on the Christian Unilit bestseller list, though it was first published in 1970 and is in its 79th printing, with over 600,000 copies in print. The book is "a lively, interesting, devotional commentary on one of the best-loved Bible passages."

Another Canadian book is John White's *The Fight*, in which Christian "joy is often preceded by, and mysteriously intertwined with struggle."

*Jesus, By John,* "a beautiful and devotional study of Jesus—as John saw Him," is by Paul B. Smith, minister of the fundamentalist People's Church in Willowdale, Ontario.

In the realm of personal testimonial, Lee Bryant's *The Magic Bottle* reflects her deep concern for women with drinking problems.

Every year in July, the Christian Booksellers Association in Canada holds its convention somewhere in central Canada. Although extremely impressive, it is definitely a poor cousin to the giant Christian Booksellers Association Convention in the United States. The U.S. CBA convention features dress-up characters such as Preacher Pigeon (a four-colour take off on Big Bird from Sesame Street) and Barney the Bear (a character in Spire Comic Books) which are geared exclusively to the Christian marketplace.

The CBA Convention is more than a book fair. Only half of the booths actually exhibit books. The others display greeting cards and gift wrapping inscribed with religious messages, Bible verses and quotations carved into burnt-wood placques, art objects, bumper stickers and even a booth with a rack of small comic-book evangelical diatribes or tracts, aimed particularly at teenagers, with titles such as *Hit Parade* or *Jesus Bats 1000.* One often finds these tracts strategically discarded on subway or bus seats.

Conventions are usually thought to be a time for rounds of free booze in the hospitality suite, business wheeling and dealing and even an extra-marital fling. But the CBA conventions are markedly different.

The first difference is that most buyers (the bookstore owners and staff) attend the week-long convention with their wives or husbands. Quite a few of the stores are "mom and pop" operations and children are welcome at the convention.

For $6.00 a day, parents can send each of their little ones

off to day camp for the week. Every morning they are bused to a camp outside of town and returned for the evening's activities, which include magic shows, ventriloquists and Bible Study sessions.

Parents are not short of extra-curricular organized activities. There are day trips by bus to local evangelical book distributors or publishers; tours of 100 Huntley Street and sightseeing around town.

Every morning begins with breakfast devotions at 7:45 a.m. sharp. Luncheons feature live entertainment and hymn-sings, and dinner is also an upbeat affair. The speeches range from personal testimonials to witnessing of faith. And everyone goes to bed early.

"In North America, the religious book market sells between $400 and $500 million worth of books a year," said Glen Cameron of the CBA. And big sales is the name of the game on the convention floor.

Throughout the day, simultaneous with the trade fair, the Christian Booksellers Association runs seminars on marketing, financial planning, promotion and general pep talks for bookstore managers. There is an impressive emphasis on professionalism and upgrading of part-time homespun operations. Merchandise and merchandising are extremely important. At the 1982 convention in Hamilton, Ontario, member bookstore managers were treated to a seminar on how to sell choir robes.

At the 1980 convention at the Sheraton Centre in Toronto, the Anglican Book Centre and CANEC, the publishing division of the United Church of Canada, joined the 70-or-so exhibitors. It was their first CBA convention and Archie Johnstone, then marketing and purchasing manager for CANEC, said it was probably the last. "We came into the trade show to see what kind of a reaction we would get. But it's a gimmicky sort of fair. Only three booths had solely book displays. For instance, the Anglican Book Centre (ABC) had excellent quality books at their booth but got little attention. We try to be ecumenical and that is very hard in today's market."

Emrys Jenkins, the director of marketing for the Division of Communications of the United Church of Canada, echoed Johnstone's dissatisfaction. "I don't think we were even invited back there. We have had to identify our market and it just isn't the evangelical bookstores. The United Church has bookstores in Edmonton, Winnipeg, Toronto and Moncton. We are never in the downtown core, like the evangelical bookstores, and we do 80-85 percent of our sales by mail.

"We have a different type of market; our market is thoughtful, liberal and interested in social action. As a result we are not as ambitious as other publishers are. It's too risky. We only publish books for the United Church."

How are mainline church sales? Comparative figures aren't available.

*No Two Alike* by Betty Jane Wylie is a collection of faith stories by church lay people from across the country. In ten months it sold 6000 copies at about $5.00.

Another good seller is *Living Between Memory and Hope*, which is a "Bible Study for Today" with a missionary emphasis It sold 10,000 in the 18 months following its release at $6.95.

Jenkins comments, "We have increased our total sales by over 12 percent from last year. The average in the retail book market was only 10 percent. I guess we are doing well."

Although perhaps intended as a gesture of coming-together, the CANEC and Anglican Book Centre participation in the 1980 convention further widened the rift between "mainline" church publishing and their evangelical counter-parts.

While CANEC and the Anglican Book Centre had a good selection of thoughtful and positive books on faith and society, evangelical publishers concentrated on individual testimonials and exposes of the ills wrought by the "humanist" outreach programmes sponsored by mainline churches.

One dissatisfied convention-goer summed up his experience this way: "The evangelical publishers are trying to tell me I'm not a true Christian if I'm a mainliner. That sort of cuts off discussion, doesn't it?"

# 9

# Christ or Chaos in Confederation

"I consider myself a street preacher in the electronic age," Ken Campbell said by way of introduction when he came to an interview in my office in Toronto one bright fall day. "I am a sort of a 'Jeremiah' out in the marketplace protesting the ridiculing in education and the media of the proven socially superior and spiritually satisfying ways of the Lord; I expect to be the target for some verbal tomatoes and eggs."

Taking my hand in a warm tight grip, he reminded me not of Jeremiah but of Stewart Granger. But instead of a cowboy outfit, Campbell is neatly and casually dressed in a vanilla jacket and tie, and a dark brown shirt and pants. His red-gold hair, jauntily blown dry to the right side, is threaded with grey.

Nearing 50, Ken Campbell is probably the veteran of more Christian crusades, more TV interview shows, and more public meetings on issues from gay rights to smut, than any other Canadian evangelical preacher.

Born in Hartford, Ontario, the son of a Baptist minister, Campbell was "saved" at 18. After high school in Oshawa, Ontario, he set out for William Jennings Bryan (of the "Monkey Trial" fame) Christian College in Dayton, Tennessee. He graduated with a bachelor of arts degree in history and returned to Milton, Ontario with the American bride he had met at college. To this day, he has no formal degree in theology. In 1960, a tragic car accident took his wife's life and left him with two small daughters, aged three and 17 months, to care for.

"You know, I got many condolence notes at that time," Campbell recalled. "But just one stuck in my mind. It was from a classmate of my wife's from Denver, Colorado. She had had spinal polio and doctors said she'd never walk out of that hospital. But she did, and within a few months she joined me in Milton and we have been very happy." Norma and Ken were married and had three more children.

Annette, the eldest, is working on her doctorate in church history; Jennie, a year younger, is hoping to enrol in graduate studies at Hebrew University in Jerusalem. The middle son and daughter are students at Jerry Falwell's Liberty Baptist College in Lynchburg, Virginia. Falwell is a special friend of their dad's. The youngest daughter, Shelly, is finishing high school at The People's Christian School, a private school offshoot of the fundamentalist People's Church in Willowdale, Ontario. It costs $150 a month plus school busfare of $50 for Campbell to send Shelly to that school but he says it's worth every cent. His children used to attend the local public high school until Campbell recognized his "duty as a Christian and as a taxpayer."

"My wife wept after perusing a novel my daughter brought home from high school," explains Campbell. "These youngsters shouldn't have to sift through recommended 'literary sewage' in search of the ennobling and beautiful of great literature." He hearkens back to the days when he was in high school and classics such as Shakespeare were read from expurgated high school editions without the "offensive gutter language."

The book that made Norma cry was John Updike's *Rabbit Redux*.

That was just the start. Soon after, four members of a gay liberation group from McMaster University spoke at a grade twelve health class on human sexuality; Campbell saw red.

When Campbell received his property tax bill, he withheld

part of the payment as a protest against "moral pollution" in the public education system, estimating the high school education portion of his taxes at about $100. He says he was prepared to lose his house or go to jail to break the school board's stranglehold which amounted to "sexual fascism" or "totalitarian secularism."

While school board officials and some teachers called Campbell's accusations "a tempest in a teapot," many ratepayers in the Halton region west of Toronto were sympathetic to Campbell.

"When it comes to sex education in the schools," Campbell told me, "the government imposes a completely secular philosophy. It assumes the myths of Darwin and of Freud. Darwin says all we are is appetites and Freud says our only sin is that we repress ourselves. In a pluralistic society like ours, there should be two streams in education from kindergarten to grade twelve at least. One would be the Progressive Stream, basically what we have now, and one would be the Traditional Stream which would be based on the Judeo-Christian principles. Parents should have a choice."

What some people called a tempest in a teapot got many of Halton region's 220,000 citizens boiling. In the late 70s, more than a thousand people turned out at a rally in Milton to hear Campbell speak. The Halton Renaissance Committee was born. From there, Renaissance committees sprang up across the country. The head office in Milton, Renaissance International became a registered charity with contributions being tax deductible.

In 1979, Renaissance sponsored hearings across Canada on behalf of the Renaissance "Commission on the Family." Dr. Blair Shaw, a practising psychologist, formerly of Oakville, Ontario and now living in Lunenburg, Nova Scotia, was appointed chairman of the "Commission on the Family." Unlike Campbell, Dr. Shaw had little interest in seeing religion being taught in the schools. "The Lord's prayer should not be compulsory for all students because the

schools are supposed to serve such a wide range of beliefs,"
Shaw commented when I interviewed him. He added that
children are "forced to memorize ritualistic prayers that most
Bishops would call 'bull' if you gave them a shot of Canadian
Club whiskey at the beginning." He did agree with Campbell
that sex education must be the preserve of the family.
Children are "force-fed sexual attitudes which are the
family's role to teach. Sexual mores and customs have no
damn business in the schools."

Shaw travelled across the country listening to deputations
and speeches from parents, educators, clergymen and others
on ideas to boost the image and the popularity of the family.

The cost of the commission was underwritten by hundreds
of concerned Canadians who sent in monthly pledges of five
to ten dollars. According to Campbell's printed broadsheet
*Encounter*, Dr. Shaw was making a "vital contribution" as
the spokesman "for all free men and parents, particularly in
eye-balling this wicked anti-Christian arrogance in high
places in our society." *Encounter* is comprised mainly of
articles reprinted from the right-wing tabloid the *Toronto
Sun* and of appeals for funds larded with the usual quotations
from Scripture.

Unfortunately, Shaw ran afoul of quite a few of those
people in high places. Once a highly successful and
well-to-do psychologist with private practices in Oakville
and in Mississauga, Ontario, he was effectively drummed out
of business and financially ruined by the "liberal establish-
ment," according to Campbell. He lost one of his major
contracts with a local school board, was invited to speak
publicly on fewer and fewer platforms and was no longer
accepted as a regular contributor to several syndicated
newspaper columns on psychology.

Undaunted, he found work on an Indian reserve in
northwestern Ontario and moved his family there to start
again. A year later they moved to the Maritimes. "In fact, he
was persecuted for his beliefs on the family," claims

Campbell. "The risks—financial and otherwise in our type of business—are pretty steep."

"Parents have a prior right to choose the kind of education that shall be given to their children," Campbell shouted across the table at me. "Now I didn't make that up. It's from the United Nations Universal Declaration of Human Rights, Article 26." Even in a small conference room, Campbell carries on as if he were delivering the Sermon on the Mount.

"What choice do we as parents actually have? Parents think cars are more important than kids."

He saw my look of surprise and jumped in.

"If Trudeau said tomorrow that the only car available in Canada was going to be the Volkswagen from now on, just how long do you think his government would last? Well, that is what the government is telling us in regard to our children and their education. It's either the public schools or the Catholic separate schools. It's either 'lex rex' or 'rex lex.'" He grinned, waiting for my response.

"What do you mean?"

"Well either the law is king, or the king is law and I know that I want our King to be law." His eyes twinkled upward.

"But you don't have to be religious to believe that we need the voucher system to make the educational system in this province fair," he said, changing the topic. "Here is a column by Michele Landsberg in the *Toronto Star*. She is the wife of Stephen Lewis, the former leader of the Ontario New Democratic Party. Even she endorses the voucher system."

In her column on January 8, 1980, Landsberg had written that the voucher system was "the ultimate nose-thumbing at the state monopoly which for a century has been telling us that it knows better than we do about educating our children." She wrote that, for the first time, the voucher system would allow "real equality" in the school system.

Landsberg and Campbell would be strange bedfellows indeed. Landsberg, a committed feminist, advocate of removing abortion from the Criminal Code, a tireless booster of Planned Parenthood, and well-known NDPer and social critic, was shocked at the mileage her column on the voucher system gathered in Campbell's various publications.

"If he endorses it, I'd have to rethink it deeply," Landsberg told me in a phone interview. "I don't support him at all; nothing could be farther from the truth. He reprinted my article, without permission, at the time of the Toronto municipal election in 1980, and used it to try to defeat a local NDP candidate.

"I resent him trying to gain a spurious respectability by pretending to be endorsed by mainstream writers. I've never spoken to the man; I don't want to give him the credibility."

But Campbell launches readily into a pat explanation of the workings of the voucher system. Every parent would get a voucher from the government for each child of school age. The voucher would be worth the same amount for each student irrespective of his parents' income or social class. The parent could then take the voucher to any school that fulfills basic curriculum and physical specifications and "cash" it in toward the child's education.

"We are able to go to the Jewish community, for instance, and get them to back the idea of a voucher," said Campbell. "Take the Associated Hebrew Schools in North York. They were within inches of having the Ministry of Education agree to their being able to function with their own philosophy as an Alternative School but then political power was brought to bear. No public funds for religious schools, they were told. That is completely crazy when Roman Catholics get to send their kids to publicly funded Catholic schools to grade ten [now, grade 13] for *free*..."

Rabbi Irwin Witty, executive director of the Board of Jewish Education in Toronto, said he was being kind to Campbell by saying the man "is engaging in an overstatement."

Though Rabbi Witty had never met or spoken to Campbell, he had heard of Renaissance International and its reputation. "We're not against morality or ethics. I have the impression that Campbell is part of the movement to veto what does and doesn't work in education. No one I know in the Jewish community is prepared to underscore by legislation religious or moral limitations. I don't think we'd be partners in that.

"We don't dictate. We follow the province's general studies curriculum in all of our schools."

Arthur Tannenbaum, administrator of the Associated Hebrew Schools of Toronto, was more direct. "Evangelist or not, we have nothing in common. I wouldn't even talk to the man. We work through the Ontario Association for Alternative and Independent Schools, which is an umbrella group. I don't deal with individual organizations or lobby groups."

But it didn't seem to register with Campbell that those in a similar situation to his wanted nothing to do with him or his supporters. When I asked how the $3000 or so voucher could possibly pay for a student's education in a small school with limited enrolment, Campbell became impatient. "These things can all be ironed out," he assured me. Where would the teachers come from and how could a parent be sure they were qualified? "Well," he sniffed, "a Christian teacher shouldn't be forced to teach in a school system based on secular humanism, that is, where man, not God, is supreme. So right now teachers are being discriminated against. I think you would find with the voucher system the teachers would teach at schools where they would be the most happy and sympathetic to the needs of the students and parents."


Campbell dons another hat. The tireless, battle-scarred itinerant evangelist becomes, first the chairman of the Halton Renaissance Committee, and then head of "Renaissance

International," an organization that exists only in Canada. He is editor of *Encounter*, an "independent quarterly speaking to, and for, the evangelical Christian." He edits *Liberation*, a newsprint broadsheet published by "Renaisance International" for Metro Toronto's "Moderate Majority". . . "representing the civilized concerns of the silent majority, and the civil rights of the silent minorities." Campbell is also president of Richmond College, a Christian liberal arts college in Milliken, Ontario. Some of his empire-building has gotten him into hot water.

In 1980, ten days after the Toronto municipal election, Campbell received a letter from Revenue Canada which proposed that the govenment take away Renaissance's religious tax status. Renaissance is a registered religious charity with a stated aim of "Propagating the values and philosophy of our Judeo-Christian heritage—the foundation of a free and responsible society."

In an article on Campbell in Toronto's *Globe and Mail*, the suggestion was made that the reason for the possible revoking of Renaissance's charitable status was its distribution, during the 1980 civic elections, of a booklet which accused specific candidates of blackening the name of "Toronto the Good" by supporting the issue of homosexual rights. I asked Campbell about it.

"Well," he said, not missing a beat, "I have a year's issues of the United Church *Observer* sitting in my house right now. I'll be glad to show in court that every page is about politics. If the government de-registers us, then the same will have to go for the United Church, the Anglican Church and many more. We'll appeal it to the top."

On November 9, 1980, the day before the Toronto municipal election, Renaissance International had bought a $4000 ad, centrespread in the *Toronto Sun*. The ad stated: "Metro's Moderate Majority Urges All Eligible Voters in Metro Toronto Concerned for the Future of Freedom and the Family to Vote for Toronto the Good not San Francisco North." It urged voters not to endorse the socially destructive objectives of the national campaign by radical militant homosexuals to make Canada their "closet." It went on to name what Renaissance called "the Gang of Nine," nine trustees of the Toronto Board of Education who voted against considering a motion "banning homosexual proselytizing in the schools."

Campbell's jump in logic catapulted him into the realm of demagogy. "Thus it may be interpreted that the following Nine Trustees are in favour of homosexuality being preached to our children as a normal alternative sexual orientation." In print he named the trustees and the wards they represented.

One bit of hodge-podge lists "Facts, not Fiction" about homosexuals and urges them to repent while they still have time. Another box is entitled "Mayor Sewell Slanders All Legitimate Minorities." Campbell wrote that the then-mayor slandered them by lumping them in the same pudding as "flaunting homosexuals." Another bit contained a diatribe against then-Trustee Bob Spencer. Campbell accused him of blaspheming Christ by making intemperate remarks and, after a long Bible quote, called for an apology or a motion of censure. Finally, the most vitriolic statement of all: "Obviously the militant homosexuals have obtained everything for which they have been lobbying or you would have heard them screaming. You would apparently rather please perverts than parents."

But Ken Campbell says he loves homosexuals. "I have nothing against them, in fact, like all God's creatures, I love them. Of course they are sinners and have to repent. It's the militant ones I'm against." This last category includes men like George Hislop, entrepreneur and former aldermanic candidate in Toronto's Ward 6. Campbell believes Hislop was responsible for what amounts to "ratting" on Renaissance to Revenue Canada. "I want to know how a militant homosexual crusader, masquerading as an aldermanic candidate, by his unfounded, widely publicized charges against a pro-family religious charity can apparently instigate immediate de-registration action by a government agency against that charity?" Campbell wrote in yet another more recent newspaper ad.

"We don't know to this day what we've done wrong," he insists. "Technically the government has never contacted us to explain what we've done that is incompatible with our charitable status."

In November 1982, the federal court of appeal restored Renaissance's charity status on the grounds that Campbell had been denied the natural justice of a proper hearing.

By the time it was over, Campbell had to fork out $20,000 in legal expenses, and expects to get only $2000 back, even though the government department has been assessed some of Campbell's costs. But it was all worth it. Campbell says he scored a victory for the public good. "Revenue Canada must now hold a hearing to decide whether it is going to give or revoke charity status. They do not have discretionary power."

The ruling, and thus the government, did not deal with the heart of the matter: can religious organizations like Renaissance (or the mainstream churches) engage in political activity and hold charity status?

Both emphasize there is a convergence between morality and politics; they differ in moral issues they choose to tackle. Ken Campbell can continue to buy his ads with tax free dollars.

"Should religious institutions be involved in advocacy?" Ken Ward, assistant treasurer of the United Church of Canada, asks rhetorically. "The response would be 'certainly.' When we see laws that need to be changed, the church should and does speak up forcefully. We don't see ourselves in politics. We are dealing with morality."

Campbell is more restrictive about what constitutes morality. "I draw a distiction between the appropriateness of the religious presence as a prophetic voice, and as a political voice seeking to impose its political agenda."

Actually each religious grouping has its own political agenda. The mainstream churches worry about native land claims, South African apartheid, events in Latin America and disarmament. And Ken Campbell has no compunction about intervening in a Toronto municipal election. His latest target is church peace activists whom he describes as "blasphemous."

He has helped set up the Heritage Forum as an alternative to the Canadian Council of Churches' position on the escalating arms race. "I would characterize it as an interchurch council articulating the centrist view of Christianity." He describes the Forum's position as "peace through prayer and proper preparation."

Campbell supports U.S. President Ronald Reagan's "peace through strength" policy against the Soviet Union, citing Romans 13 in the Bible to bolster it. "God established a state to restrain the lawless. It is the obligation of the state to restrain the gangster elements internally and internationally."

Campbell, in the spring of 1983, spoke out against the showing of the Oscar-winning anti-nuclear National Film Board documentary *If You Love this Planet* at a Richmond Hill (a town near Toronto) high school.

"Anti-American propaganda in an Ontario high school is as inappropriate to a moderate majority as is anti-Semitism in Eckville, Alberta." He spoke in his own rhetorical style.


Ken Campbell had been gleeful when I called him to arrange our interview. "I have great news. Jerry Falwell is coming on a tour across Canada. I just took out an ad in the *Toronto Star* and we'll be notifying people across the country." The ad announced "The Christ or Chaos in Confederation Crusade...one night only in Toronto's magnificent New Roy Thomson Hall, November 16, 1982."

There were to be 2812 free seats to be reserved for members of a "sponsors club."

Falwell is a personal friend of Campbell's. He wrote the

introduction for Campbell's book, *No Small Stir*, published in 1980. Falwell shoots from the hip. "He [Campbell] wants to do for Canada what the Moral Majority is beginning to do for America—call the nation back to God. . . . Everywhere I go in 'the land of the Maple Leaf,' people tell me they face the same subtle problems as in the States. The attack of the enemy of righteousness is the same on both sides of the border."

I was not the first person to suspect that Campbell's Renaissance International is a branch office for Falwell's Moral Majority.

"Renaissance is not the Moral Majority's Canadian Wing," counters Campbell. "On the contrary, Renaissance is a grass-roots, 'home-grown' Canadian movement, crusading within the Canadian social-religious-political structures for faith, family and freedom. While there is much I hold in common with my friend, Dr. Jerry Falwell, of commitments to radical Christian discipleship, the Renaissance strategies are distinctively and appropriately Canadian."

While Falwell was slated to speak only in Toronto and Edmonton, he was sending a dozen Liberty Baptist Singers to 25 cities on the tour.

Touring is old hat for Campbell. As an itinerant preacher for 23 years, he travelled about half of each year across the country. Accompanied by gospel musician Jim Reese, the Campbell-Reese Evangelistic Association ("a small Billy Graham-type crusade," says Campbell modestly) averaged 25 crusades every year. That time on the road netted Campbell a mailing list of over 50,000 across Canada.

Talk of the Christ or Chaos Crusade brought back exciting memories. Campbell has largely retired from travel: he is pastor of Emmanuel Baptist Church in Milton, Ontario. "It's my home congregation and my home town since 1958," he told me proudly. "They know me there and I feel they can tell me if they don't like something I'm doing."

When he left my office he was going to work on another ad—this time for the *Toronto Star*'s religion page, headed

"How to Liberate Your Children: The Doctrines of Demons which Dominate Public Education in Ontario."

# 10

# The Anti-Abortion Connection

There were no empty seats at the Alberta Physicians for Life banquet held in April 1982 at Edmonton's Hotel MacDonald. Over 800 doctors and their wives, political figures and would-be politicians, crowded into the faded elegance of the Tonquin Room with its flocked wallpaper and thinly upholstered chairs to hear one of the top anti-abortion crusaders of the United States. Bernard Nathanson, M.D., a New York obstetrician and gynecologist, was in fine form.

Nathanson was visiting Calgary and Edmonton to fire up the spirits of the anti-abortion movement and give it some much-needed ammunition to do battle with what he calls, "the liberal college-educated press."

McGill-educated Nathanson has the credentials. He is the co-founder of NARAL, the National Association for the Repeal of Abortion Laws, the American big brother to CARAL, the Canadian organization. He is also former director of the New York Centre for Reproductive and Sexual Health (CRASH), touted as the largest abortion clinic in the world. During his year-and-a-half tenure as its director, Nathanson claims he presided over some 75,000 abortions. And then he made a complete about-face.

In 1979, Nathanson's book *Abortion America* was published. The book, describing his personal odyssey from prominent abortionist to "pro-life" advocate, was first published by Doubleday and Co., Inc. But the copy I picked up at his press conference was published by Life Cycle Books, a "Christian publishing house" in Toronto. Despite his claims of having no political or religious axe to grind, Nathanson regularly works the born-again circuit; all the more interesting when he explains in *Abortion America* that he was born a Jew and is now an avowed atheist. He has spoken on many Right to Life platforms throughout the U.S. and Canada and his book (the Life Cycle edition) is widely distributed through evangelical bookstores and Bible Study groups. Nathanson shrugs off the connection.

Canadian Physicians for Life, the parent of Alberta Physicians for Life which sponsored the dinner, is a ginger group within the Canadian Medical Association. The master of ceremonies was Dr. Walter Kazun, President of Canadian Physicians for Life, a Vancouver general practitioner, father of four and grandfather of six. Most of the mint parfait desserts had been removed and the coffee cups refilled by the time Dr. Kazun took great pleasure in introducing Philip Ketchum, a key member of St. Paul's Anglican Church in Edmonton. Ketchum had invited Mustard Seed, a group of evangelical actors, singers and dancers from his church, to entertain the gathering with a play entitled "God's Gift."

Nathanson shifted uncomfortably as the earnest Dr. Kazun outlined what we were about to see. "This is an original work," stressed Kazun with a smile, "I'm sure you'll all recognize the pantomine. Three young girls are going from maidenhood to motherhood." Smiling and approving faces shone up at him from the audience. He went on, "The young girls meet their young men, fall in love and the kiss represents the honeymoon." Giggles rippled through the crowd. "The nine months pass rather quickly and a child is born to each couple," he finished brightly. Applause from the audience. I was ready for the worst.

But Mustard Seed's performance was polished and smooth. The dance, choreographed by Ketchum's wife Margaret, was set to music composed for Psalm 139.

As the women went through the rituals, a chorus sang:


*Search me, O my God, and know my heart;*
*Search me, O my God, and know my anxious thoughts;*
*Search me, O my God, and cleanse my ways;*
*Lead me in the Way everlasting.*


*When I sit, and when I rise,*
*When I go out, or close my eyes,*
*Speaking truth or telling lies,*
*You know me, O Lord.*


*If I go to the heavens, I will find You there;*
*O where from Your presence can I flee?*
*If I rise on the wings of the early dawn,*
*And fly far away 'cross the sea,*
*Your hand is the hand that will be my guide,*
*Your right hand is holding me.*


The audience was spellbound—all except for Dr. Nathanson and his wife, Adele. Sitting patiently at the head table, he made notes along the edges of his prepared speech while she turned to stare glumly at the stage behind her.

After the three main dancers took their bows, they joined the rest of the group at the piano on the side of the stage. The soloist sang another original song based on Job 38-39, "Miracles I made for You," while the other nine joined the refrain.


*Where were you when I laid the cornerstone in place?*
*Tell me if you understand the meaning of my Grace?*
*Who was there to set the limits for the changing time?*

*Miracles I've made for you to fill your life with peace.*
*Have you seen the frost and snow which comes from up*
*above.*
*Miracles I've made for you, it's my gift of love—*


Dr. Kazun thanked Mustard Seed and asked for a round of applause. The troupe smiled their thanks at the chance to perform and disappeared down into the audience to take their seats.

Kazun then introduced Dr. Fawzy Morcos of the Alberta chapter of Physicians for Life. Morcos is an obstetrician and gynecologist at Misericordia Hospital in Edmonton.

He brought a slide show of one statistical table after another—some in large type, others compressed from government sources—that showed how serious the abortion situation is: the number of abortions exceeds the number of live births in some areas, the government lacks concern; the hospitals are having to fight to retain their prerogative not to set up Therapeutic Abortion Committees (TACs).


Currently across Canada, abortions can be performed legally only in hospitals that have a TAC set up. Therapeutic Abortion Committees are usually comprised of three staff doctors who are supposed to judge the case of each pregnant woman (as explained by herself or her doctor, acting as representative) and decide whether her request for abortion is within the scope of the legislation that allows abortion under certain limited medical circumstances.

In his book, Nathanson caustically outlines just how the average woman who came to his practice in the U.S. could easily negotiate an abortion on medical grounds.

Nathanson writes: "The Psychiatric Harlequinade of 1969 began, and the script—unvarying and after a few months, boring—went something like this."

"Doctor, are you sure I'm pregnant?"

"No question about it."

"I simply can't have this baby. I:
a) am not married
b) don't have the money
c) can't disgrace my parents
d) can't have my husband find out
e) am not ready to be a mother."

"Well, if you're really desperate about this, I mean to the point of SUICIDE or something, then if you were to see a couple of psychiatrists who would attest to that, we could terminate the pregnancy for you."

"Oh yes—anything. Whom shall I see and how soon can I see them?"

"Out would come the little notebook from my back pocket for a quick consultation to see which two I had sent the last woman to.....and I would pick a pair I hadn't used in a while. Their letters in hand, I would make my appearance at the weekly Grand Guignol."

Nathanson explains in the book that at one time the letters from the psychiatrists were detailed and serious attempts to explain the psychopathology involved. But by the time the 1970s arrived, those letters deteriorated.

"The committees were not only aware of the gathering political force of the abortion movement that year, but, having approved the first few abortions on psychiatric grounds, they knew they could hardly reject the next hundred when the letters came from the same staff psychiatrists, couched in the same ominous though opaque psycho-jargon....The members (of the TAC) struggled bravely until the liberal abortion law passed the legislature and then quietly yielded up the ghost."

Morcos continued to shout Canadian facts and figures. By the end of Morcos' presentation, the room was positively steaming with the combined rage of the staunch anti-abortion doctors and their wives. When Kazun reminded him of the time limit, he snapped off the projector and told the crowd that a financial contribution to the Department of Obstetrics and Gynecology of the Misericordia Hospital—marked to his attention—would secure a tape-cassette of the evening's speeches. Wiping his forehead, he sat down. The people at the tables shifted nervously—aware that his shrill voice and carrying on, though unprofessional, was just what the doctor ordered to rekindle those embers of disgust, anger and punishment which often accompany discussion on abortion.

After Kazun's introduction, Nathanson, too, was bullish. But where Morcos was merely emotional, Nathanson was the consummate professional—at times witty, at times bitingly sardonic—in short, elegant. A squat vigorous-looking man of 56, Nathanson is into his third marriage and his third decade as an obstetrician. Whenever he cited examples which had occurred in the States, he added he was sure it was "all the same up here." No one argued.

Nathanson brought his own hard-hitting slide show, based on his experience in NARAL: "How Permissive Abortion Was Sold to the American Public." He prefaced the first slide with, "We sold abortion to the States with hardball, ruthless politics. The Planned Parenthood empire is the most dangerous organization we're up against."

The audience grunted their agreement and, as the lights went down, the shimmer from the screen caught the tiny gold pair-of-feet lapel pins worn by the more militant anti-abortionists at the tables.

Each slide contained a written message. Nathanson's verbal clarifications sharpened the subtitles.

"How was permissive abortion sold to the American public?" he asked. "I'll tell you how. Next slide."

*Anti-Catholicism has historically been a subtle but*

*productive political tactic of the liberal camp,"* the screen blinked.

"You know," Nathanson said confidently, "I call anti-Catholicism the anti-Semitism of the intellectual." Approving nods at my table. Next slide.

*Denigrate the scientific evidence which shows that life begins at conception. Insist when life begins is a theological/legal/ethical/philosophical issue. Anything but a scientific one.*

*Capture the media. This is a particularly effective tactic for liberal causes in that the megapress (the national press) is irredeemably liberal.*

Nathanson's voice interrupted. "Here is a slide of one of our NARAL leaflets. Notice the virulent and poisonous anti-Catholic bias. This is a profile of our opposition." Next slide. "You know my new book is coming out soon. It's called *The Abortion Papers*. It will be out in about nine months. It takes about nine months for anything good to come about." Gales of laughter in the audience. Next slide.

*Make the public realize it's not a religious issue. It's a moral and a national issue.*

Nathanson barked, "What are the solutions? Look at these slides."

*Solutions: Make certain that the recent new data, facts, information and revelations from the new explosive science of fetology (study of the fetus) are made public. Do not allow the argument to deteriorate into the now obsolete lines of the 1960s and early 70s. Demand that the media report our position fairly. Emphasize the scientific knowledge concerning the fetus; its human characteristics as shown on ultrasound, intra-uterine surgery, intra-uterine transfusion.*

By memory, Nathanson listed fifty different life-saving operations that could be done on the fetus in the womb.

His voice shot out of the darkness, "You know the *New York Times* is the most notorious pro-abortion rag in the U.S.? But even *they* have had articles such as 'Saving Babies Before Birth,' which explain these types of operations on the fetus to enable it to live. Or it reports on the Obstetrics and Gynecological newspaper's article 'Pregnancy Early in Life Might Avert Later Cancer.' No woman who has seen her baby on an ultra-sound screen moving, breathing and sucking its thumb can fail to be profoundly moved by the experience. Make a preliminary ultra-sound a mandatory part of the informed consent for abortion—with the screen turned IN FULL VIEW for the mother!"

Wild applause from the audience. Next slide.

*How the media have trashed and misreported our position. The media must be called to account and be chastened. Their house must be cleaned up.*

Nathanson intones, "In the *New York Times* article 'Senate Hearings on Abortion Close on Emotional Note'—I wasn't even MENTIONED and I was a witness! The media is not to be trusted. It's corrupt and wicked. Next."

*Why do they take the liberal stance? Who are the media? Robert Lichter and Stanley Rothman showed their findings in a report, 'The Media and the Business Elite,' in December 1981.*

The slide flashed a chart and Nathanson summarized: "They interviewed 247 of the media elite in the U.S. on their presidential voting record and found, in 1968, only 13 reported voting for Nixon, while 87 voted for Humphrey. In 1972, only 19 voted for Nixon while 81 voted for McGovern. And that year was a *landslide victory* for Nixon. In 1976, only 19 voted for Ford and 81 voted for Carter."

The next slide, another chart.

Nathanson carried on. "This survey of the same group shows the media elite's attitude to societal questions. For instance, the statement that the woman has the right to decide on abortion—90 percent agreed strongly with that statement. 'Homosexuality is wrong.' Seventy-six percent disagreed with that statement."

I heard a couple of clucks from my table mates.

"'Homosexuals shouldn't teach in the public schools.' Eighty percent disagreed with that. And, most telling of all—the statement 'Adultery is wrong.' Only 54 percent of the media elite agreed with that! And you know that 95 percent of them are male and 79 percent are white!"

He went on.

"How do we counter a media like this? They are in favour of abortion; they are against prayer in the schools; they are for busing. Next slide."

*Solutions:*
*1. Monitor the Megapress.*
*2. Letters to the Editor*
*3. Threaten to boycott the products of their major advertisers.*
*4. Threaten a move to set professional qualifications and standards for journalists. Professional licensing if necessary.*

Nathanson was riding high. "No one tells the press to shape up and conform. You know in places like Europe and Argentina, the press has to be licensed. Why not? As a professional doctor I have to be licensed!" Next slide.

*5. No minorities represented in the media elite.*
*6. We need a true watchdog as well as an acceptable alternative to the privately owned megapress.*

"I believe we need a public newspaper system similar to the Public Broadcasting System in television and radio. It would be funded in part by the government and partly through private grants," he explained. Rumbles throughout the audience. "Like your CBC." Groans from the assembly.

Nathanson noted their reaction and passed on to the next slide. "Now look at this. I stole this," he said proudly. "When I left the clinic, I took a lot of papers with me and let's just say this one fell into my lap. This is the private income tax form filed by the New York City chapter of Planned Parenthood. It's supposed to be a non-profit organization. The form required the organization to list any professionals that work full-time with the outfit. See all these doctors' names? I know and have worked with many of them and I know they are lying when they say they work *only* for Planned Parenthood earning *only* this amount. Most of them had staff jobs at hospitals, or were only consultants. Only *part* of their incomes came from the organization.

"So you see what we are up against with Planned Parenthood? And you see what major private sources of income they receive. The Rockefeller Foundation, $650,000," he read off the slide, "the Mellons, $250,000 and the Ford Foundation, $500,000."

The nattily dressed man beside me whispered, "Just think of *that* the next time you buy a car!"

"Well," sighed Nathanson. "All this will be exposed in my forthcoming book. They'll see." Cheers from the audience.

His last slide lit up the screen. It was a handwritten letter, neatly signed.

"Now for the *piece de resistance*," Nathanson said. "This letter is from one Jill Upshaw, who *used* to be a patient in my private practice.

"For anyone who can't decipher her writing, she says that in view of my heretical stand on abortion and my public activities on that issue, she can no longer be a patient of mine."

Some people in the audience oohed and ahhed their surprise. "But you know what? I don't give a damn. Good riddance to patients like her, I say! Good evening, ladies and gentlemen." With a flourish he held up his arms in the V for victory posture and stood before the microphone while the lights went on in the hall. The audience, table by table, rose to their feet in a standing ovation.

As Dr. Kazun stood to thank Nathanson formally, he unfolded a piece of paper and read out the names of the organizations that helped Physicians for Life arrange the dinner and meeting. The list included Campaign Life, the wives of the Physicians for Life, The Voice of the Unborn, the Catholic Women's League, the Knights of Columbus, Catholic Communication, Central Pentecostal Church, the Alberta Association of Women United for Families.

Nathanson sat impassively as the organizations were trotted out and thanked. Doctors' wives rushed him at his table to autograph their books.

Earlier that day, Nathanson held a press conference in the hotel.

"Why did you change your position on the question of abortion?" asked one young woman journalist.

"Well, I believe my change of heart was an evolution of thinking. It parallelled the science of fetology—the study of the fetus. Back in the late 1960s, we didn't know what we do today about the life of the fetus. Our research on the fetus has left no doubt in anyone's mind that a fetus is a person and a human being." Nathanson's hands were folded in front of him and he was talking to the woman as if she were a troublesome patient in his office.

She persisted. "But when exactly is that? At conception, at six weeks...?"

He smiled wolfishly. "There is no Bar Mitzvah in the uterus." Giggles from the Right to Life supporters in the back row. "Pro-abortion liberals have tried to set a date when the fetus becomes a human being. But I believe that is a muddle-headed way of thinking. No one questions when life ceases; no one has fixed a time for when death occurs."

She wouldn't let go. "Well, what about brain waves and electro-..."

He dismissed her question with a shrug. "Encephalogram. In general we know when death occurs. To be fair, we must define the beginning as well as the end of life. The real point no one seems to get is that abortion is a $500-million-a-year business. That money is going into the pockets of obstetricians and doctors."

Another reporter stood up. "What about abortion for a sixteen-year-old girl who has been raped—shouldn't she be allowed an abortion?"

Nathanson looked amused.

"I don't see why. Abortion is a violent act. It is an act of destruction. You don't wipe out the violence of a rape with another act of destruction.

"Many people and pro-abortionists say that in the case of rape, it is ethical to perform an abortion. But let me ask you if you know the circumstances under which you were conceived? Perhaps there was violence—we don't know. The only time that abortion is justified in my view, is when a mother's life is at stake—when there is a threat to her physical life."

The room was silent.

"I believe medical technology will diffuse the situation quite a bit. With life support systems becoming more and more sophisticated, there is no reason why we won't be able to keep the fetus alive in another woman's uterus or in a laboratory until the time of birth."

I asked: "What about those children who are deformed or have various afflictions whose mothers feel they must abort or be saddled with huge emotional and financial costs in the care of these children? If you don't allow abortion, what will become of those children?"

He thundered. "I just want to tell you what happened two weeks ago in the case of Infant Doe in Indiana." A murmer of recognition went through the room. "Infant Doe was allowed to die in the hallway of the hospital. He died of starvation! Neither the staff nor the parents were permitted to feed the infant and after five days, he died. He had Down's Syndrome, and a stomach blockage that is often associated with Down's Syndrome which can be easily repaired in surgery. But the parents did not want the surgery that would save his life.

Now there were a dozen couples in that town that put themselves on the line—they wanted to adopt that child—regardless. There are not enough children in America today to adopt: Black, White, Hispanic, disabled or anything."

You could have heard a pin drop.

"Abortion transcends all religious lines. It's not just fundamentalists that don't believe in abortion. Islam, Pentecostals, Orthodox Judaism doesn't allow it."

I asked why the tide to restrict came at a time when organized religion was gathering strength in the U.S.—wasn't it another plank in the born-again Christians' rights platform?

His eyes glared behind the glasses. "Look, I'm an atheist and have been all my adult life. Let's just say the move to criminalize abortion is gathering force. It is a part of a wave of history—of counter-revolutionary feeling—particularly in view of the destruction of human life we see."

The first reporter went back to bat. "What is your goal then?"

That was his style of question. "My goal is to stop permissive abortion. I want to narrow the grounds for the destruction of human beings. I want to see funding for better and safer contraceptives so there will be no need for abortion. I want to see a law to outlaw permissive abortions."

Several of the battle-scarred reporters begged to differ in a polite and uniquely Canadian way. Nathanson sneered his replies. He insisted that even if he got fair coverage in Edmonton, that didn't reflect the national press. When he got through, the half-dozen reporters were eating out of his hand.

The next day, the *Edmonton Journal* reprinted an article opposite the editorial page on Infant Doe in Indiana from the *Washington Post*. It seemed too much a coincidence that the day after Nathanson came to town, railing against the liberal bias of the press, the local newspaper ran a pro-life article.

# 11

# "Good and Conscientious Employees"

A few bored and resigned faces glanced up as I walked in. But most of the young people were busily working away, each in his or her own office, a three-sided wood-panelled cubicle facing the wall. An individual cardboard progress chart was taped above the narrow desk, with the supervisor's comments and performance goals clearly marked in red ink.

The supervisor sat primly in the middle of the room, knees crossed under her long table, doing her own job. When a small Canadian flag suddenly appeared on top of one of the office walls, the supervisor scuttled over to find out what the problem was. It was only a request to go to the washroom. Granted. The next flag was a question about the work. It had to wait until after lunch.

The eyes that had been watching me shifted upward slightly so they could watch the clock. It was almost lunchtime. The bell rang a few minutes later and chairs squealed away from desks as everyone got up to stretch.

The children had been hard at work since nine in the morning and needed this first break of the day. But rather than going to a cafeteria or lunchroom, they sat down again at their desks and opened their brown bag lunches.

If this sounds more like an office than a school, it is because the principal, the teachers and the parents want it this way. Welcome to Millwoods Christian School,

Edmonton, Alberta.

"We're training our students to be good and conscientious employees," explained Larry Breitkreutz, principal and self-appointed "Minister of Education." "We don't call it a classroom, we call it a 'Learning Centre'; each student has his own space, his 'office' where he is able to work independently at his own speed. When the student has a question, he raises his little flag and a supervisor will come over and discuss whatever the problem may be with him."

"Supervisor?" I asked. "Where's the teacher?"

"Well, they are teachers, or monitors, but we like to call them supervisors," he said. "They don't do any actual teaching. The books we use are self-directed, so the students work through one booklet after another in their own time. But when a student doesn't understand something in the booklet, the supervisor and he go into a small counselling room off to the side and pray about it. Usually that works."

When I arrived at the school for my tour, I was introduced to the programme and the players through a slide-tape show. "Controlled, motivated learning is the key at Millwoods Christian School," said the voice. The slide showed a cartoon drawing of a farmer riding a donkey. The farmer is carrying a whip. Suspended from a stick just ahead of the donkey is a carrot. "The driver controls, inspires and motivates the donkey," said the voice. "He sets goals which the donkey can achieve. In much the same way, a pupil must be controlled and motivated. Through quality control, a child only advances as he learns. Our programme is not permissive. Learning must be measurable and rewarded. The teacher functions as a supervisor—there is no need for a child to ask embarrassing questions in front of his peers. The child reaps the daily benefits of a private counsellor."

One of the counsellors is language arts "supervisor" Patricia Jones, a three-month veteran of Millwoods Christian School.

"I used to teach in the public school system," she explained. "And I ached when I was told I couldn't pray with my students there—even after school."

When I looked surprised she hastened to add, "Oh, well I wasn't exactly told I couldn't but I knew it would be frowned upon. There was no way of relating my faith to my students. Here, even though I am paid far less than I was paid in the public school system, I am much happier. I believe in what I am doing."

Principal Breitkreutz cut in: "We're all happier. I used to teach in junior high school. There was no discipline, no respect, and when children ran into problems with their schoolwork they just fell further and further behind. At Millwoods, our top priority is Christian character development. That means that at home and school we want to see honest, pleasant and cooperative children. I expect the girls to grow up, get married and raise Christian families. The boys must support those families. Of course some of our students will want to go on to Bible College or to serve the ministry. This school is different."

A typical day at Millwoods Christian School starts off with a Pledge of Allegiance, which sounds very familiar.

Two hundred students, ages seven to 17, and their supervisors, all dressed in scarlet and navy blue uniforms, stand at attention, right hands over their hearts and recite: "I pledge allegiance to the flag of Canada and to the country for which it stands; one nation with freedom and liberty to worship God."

Then, in unison, the students read aloud a Bible passage. They read the same passage for a month and school officials claim with pride that "by the end of the school year students have learned ten passages by memory."

After Scripture, the children sing a few Christian songs and then head for their "offices."

After lunch comes "Devotions Time" when the children engage in "social interaction in small groups." The rest of the afternoon programme features Bible Study, art, music, health classes and sports. A student who has fulfilled his weekly goals and whose behaviour is exemplary is considered to be "on privilege" and allowed to join a class field trip Friday afternoons. All students have Wednesday afternoons off.

But the real business of the school day is in the first three hours. It is here the students are put through their "Paces" learning their three "Rs." The concept of the one-room schoolhouse is still alive at Millwoods Christian School. Children from grade one to grade twelve sit at offices in the same large room; each works independently, from a series of small workbooks. The workbooks cover just five subjects: math, science, English, word-building and social studies. In each grade a subject is covered in 12 progressively more difficult workbooks. The students work through the manuals at their own pace and, with the permission of the supervisor, complete a "self-test" every few pages. They then raise their flags and ask permission from the supervisor to "score" (look up) the answers from a bank of score books, contained in a filing cabinet beside the supervisor's table in the middle of the room. Students "on privilege" don't need permission. Before any student proceeds to a higher level workbook, the supervisor administers a quiz.

ter programme of 144 "Pace" booklets is designed by d Christian Education, Inc. (A.C.E.), a group of ducators" in Lewisville, Texas. A.C.E.'s adver- e itself states its aims while admitting some of "A.C.E. does not claim theirs is the only or that it is superior to all others. They do, ality programme that vastly simplifies the opening and maintaining a Christian school with limited staff, facilities and funds."

To groups of born-again Christians across North America, desperate to set up alternative education for their children, A.C.E.'s programme is heaven-sent. The A.C.E. programme is used in hundreds of schools in the U.S., 160 in Canada and 40 in Alberta.

As a school accredited by the Alberta Department of Education, Millwoods Christian School receives 45-50 percent of the government funding that public schools get but nothing toward capital costs. The school is housed in a new, two-storey red-brick building in a middle-class suburb on Edmonton's south side. Next to the barracks-like building is a concrete beehive, The Calvary Temple, the church that founded and supports the school.

In November 1982, Calvary Temple hosted Jerry Falwell and his Liberty Baptist Singers at the 3000-seat Jubilee Auditorium in Edmonton. Behind Falwell marched an honour guard of red and blue uniformed boys from Millwoods Christian School carrying huge Canadian flags. One of the editors at the ultra-conservative Edmonton-based weekly newsmagazine *Alberta Report* told me after covering the rally: "The thing that really scared me about that outfit was those uniforms they dress the kids in. Those red shirts, dark pants and ties. When they ran across the stage at the Falwell meeting something about them reminded me of Hitler Youth."

According to Breitkreutz, parents are willing to pay about $100 a month for each child enrolled at Millwoods. They must also purchase their uniforms and pay transportation to and from the school. At $1000 a year, it is not expensive for a private school education but it is a significant sum for many families, particularly if there is more than one child. Why do they pay?

"Basic education is what we're all returning to," I explained expansively. "The public schools say all the ch' needs is within himself. Those schools emphasize discov and exploring the world around the child. When you tea

## My Goals

To learn about work, possessions, and prosperity

I. Work Is of God
  A. Work Is Not a Curse
  B. Man Must Work Hard to Provide Basic Needs

II. Our Possessions Are from God
  A. We Must Be Wise Stewards
  B. We Must Be Wise Caretakers
  C. Property Rights Are to Be Protected
  D. We Give Tithes and Offerings of Our Possessions
  E. Possessions Do Not Bring Happiness

III. What Is True Prosperity

IV. What Is an Inheritance
  A. We Receive an Inheritance from Our Parents
  B. We Have an Inheritance with Christ

To learn to use all I have for God's glory—to be generous

. . . remember the words of the Lord Jesus, how he said. It is more blessed to give than to receive. Acts 20:35

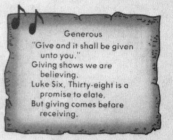

Generous
"Give and it shall be given unto you."
Giving shows we are believing.
Luke Six, Thirty-eight is a promise to elate,
But giving comes before receiving.

| autumn | else | hay | spun |
| carrot | freeze | pile | wall |
| dig | glory | seventh | wiping |

"We must remember these two very important principles that we have learned from God's Word about property. First, everything we own (property) is God's and is a gift from God; then, every man is to be a responsible steward over God's property."

Excerpts from the Grade V-VI level social studies Pace book.

All is God's.

We are responsible.

"Sometimes God does choose to give wealth in earthly goods to a Christian. That is an earthly prosperity. When a Christian is obedient to God and is generous to Him, he enjoys true prosperity within his heart. True prosperity is the peace which comes in knowing one has pleased the Lord."

Peace with God

### Generous

J. Michael mowed the yard for Pastor Gentle. He was happy to work so that he could earn some money. J. Michael finished the work, and Pastor Gentle paid him $2.00.

Later, at home, J. Michael put the money on his bed and prayed asking God how much money he should keep for himself.

When J. Michael went to church the next Sunday, he gave $1.50 of the money when the offering plate was passed. He was generous with what God had given him.

### The Pie Graph

During the month of June, Racer earned $10.00 for doing yard work. With his father's help, Racer decided to give $4.00 to the Lord at church, $1.00 to the missionary project, $.50 for an apple, $1.00 for a birthday present for a friend, and $3.50 for savings for college.

Here is a pie graph of Racer's investments. It is called a pie graph because it looks something like a cut pie.

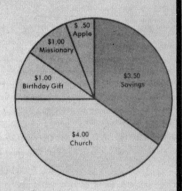

"Our minds cannot understand what being a joint-heir with Christ really means. Paul could not begin to describe for us the wonderful inheritance we have in Heaven. '. . . Eye hath not seen, nor ear heard, neither have entered into the heart of man, the things which God hath prepared for them that love him.' (I Corinthians 2:9)

"None of us can say that we should have the right to an inheritance in Heaven. None of us were members of God's family when we were born. We became children of God only because Christ bought us when He paid the price of our sin. God will allow us to enjoy a home in Heaven, yet it will cost us nothing. However, it cost Jesus Christ everything. How wonderful to know we are in God's family and as joint-heirs with Christ will receive an inheritance."

*For ye are bought with a price: therefore glorify God in your body, and in your spirit, which are God's.*
*I Corinthians 6:20*

child he's a well-developed monkey and he's going to die and rot, it can lead to social unrest, revolution and even suicide. The breakdown in society and in families does lead to suicide. And I lay the blame indirectly at the feet of our public schools. The Bible says you have to look to the word of God." The A.C.E. brochure clearly outlines the programme's goals and they aren't degrees in microbiology at MIT: "Recent surveys of approximately 400 graduates of schools using the A.C.E. programme reveal that over 80 percent chose to further their education in Christian Colleges, universities or Bible schools." Students are provided ideally with a totally "Christian environment" from cradle to graduation.

Before grade four, according to the A.C.E. curriculum, no textbooks or secondary books are used except for the Bible. From grade five up, textbooks are used sparingly. Even at the grade twelve level, Shakespeare is studied not from primary sources but as reprinted and expurgated in the "Pace" booklets.

The school's introductory filmstrip justifies the rejection of textbooks this way: "Education is not oriented around one textbook. Education is life, and the Bible is life. It is the philosophy of God's word. Children at our school learn to see life from God's point of view. Adding secondary textbooks to the Bible is like adding poison to good food."

Many educators don't like heavy reliance on textbooks. But along with the Bible, good food at Millwoods boils down to the dozen "Pace" booklets students have to ingest each year. The booklets are 8½" by 11" paperbacks with colourful covers. In grade one, students are introduced to role-model characters like Ace Virtueson, Christi Lovejoy and Pudge Meekway, children in uniforms like theirs (in the cartoons, Ace's and Pudge's red neckties have a pattern of Old Glory but the Millwoods' ties sport tiny Canadian flags), who go to an A.C.E. day school and who lead them through their "Pace" books. Adults have names like Pastor Alltruth, Pastor Gentle, Mr. Thriftmore and the supervisor "teacher," Mr. Friendson.

A typical grade five Science Pace Book begins with a Scripture verse: "I can do all things through Christ which strengtheneth me" (Philippians 4:13), and outlines what the student's goals should be. "To learn more about astronomy: 1) the outer planets; 2) telescopes; 3) meteors; 4) constellations. To learn to do all things with Jesus' help—to be confident."

A three-panel cartoon strip defines the word "confident." It shows two Black children talking: "Let's go pray for my parents to be saved." They pray and in the final panel, Pastor Gentle asks the father, "Wouldn't you like to ask Christ to forgive your sin and save you, as the Bible says?" The father replies tearfully, "Yes, I would."

At the bottom of many of the pages, the original quote from Philippians is presented incomplete with blank lines for the student to fill in missing words. By the end of the book, the student is supposed to have it memorized.

Throughout the Pace Books, comic strips highlight Christian virtues like submission, confidence in the Lord and sincerity. In a three-panel strip in the science book, Mr. Friendson, the supervisor, prays with a student in his "office": "Please, Lord Jesus, help Hapford Humblen in his Pace work today." The next panel shows the supervisor reminding Hapford, "The Bible says 'I can do all things through Christ.' Hapford Humblen, that means you!" In the final panel the supervisor emphasizes: "Remember: the person who is worse than a quitter is the person who is afraid to begin!" Hapford answers, "Yes, sir!"

Before the Pace Tests, a cartoon character tells the student: "Ask the Lord Jesus Christ to help you. Then do your best." At the end of the test, the same character is shown praying at her desk, "Thank You, Lord Jesus, for Your help."

At the end of the Science Pace Book, Mr. Friendson sums

up what the children should have learned. "By studying the heavens, we can learn much about God. The Holy Bible says, 'The heavens declare the glory of God...' (Psalm 19:1). Many other constellations are in the sky which can tell us about Jesus. These same stars have been telling about God's power and glory since the fourth day of creation. By studying astronomy, we can learn truths about our God."

What few secondary textbooks and resource books there are, can be found in Millwoods' "library." With less than a thousand books, it is small by some public school standards but Breitkreutz asked me to view it with an open mind. "The one thing I hate about you reporters is how you nitpick. Look at the whole," he commanded.

There was a set of World Book Encyclopedia, a couple of dictionaries and atlases and a lot of Bibles: Gideon Bibles, New International Version Bibles, King James Bibles, Good News Bibles, Picture Bibles, primary reader Bibles and Bibles in a short story format. There were two shelves packed with books on Bible prophecy. Half a dozen copies of Hal Lindsey's books, including *The Late Great Planet Earth* and *The 1980s: Countdown to Armageddon*, were prominent. The five shelves which featured "literature" were crammed with books few secular library users would ever see, like Don Richardson's *Lords of the Earth*, Elisabeth Elliot's *Through Gates of Splendor*, *The Cross and the Switchblade*, and *Dorie, the Girl Nobody Loved*.

*Robinson Crusoe* and a biography of Christopher Columbus were also on the shelf. "They were Christians, you know," said Breitkreutz somewhat apologetically.

"I'll bet you never saw books like these before! I've read almost all of them." He must have read my mind. "I can tell you why we don't use most of the popular novels on the shelves today. We want our novels to present a lifestyle as we want to see it. Most of today's literature shows young people rebelling against authority, young people living a promiscuous lifestyle. You become what you read, you know."

Patricia Jones, the language arts teacher who doubles as

the school librarian, backed up the principal. "I believe a book leaves an impression upon a child. Current literature tends to present an untraditional lifestyle. It promotes living a lifestyle that we'd consider unscriptural. We want our children to bring their problems through to a scriptural solution. We ask the children to turn to God and allow Him to turn their lives around. We are not interested in exposing the children to what is, but to what should be."

Jones admitted she had a tough row to hoe. "It's difficult to develop a library because of all the books we *don't want* on the shelves. But the Alberta Department of Education says appropriate reading for secondary school students means a quarter of the literature in English 10, half in English 20 and a quarter in English 30 must be Canadian content. We view literature in terms of its content and values. It might claim to be valueless but most literature is very biased."

Breitkreutz agreed. "A lot of our type of literature is kept *off* the bestseller lists. Take Francis Schaeffer's books for instance. What's the reason they've never made it to the list? Simple. His books represent a Christian view of life. Why would we want to hold up immorality, licentious behaviour and sleeping together without marriage as a model? Only books that are thoroughly immoral garbage make the bestseller list."

I half expected that. "Do you mean Margaret Atwood, Margaret Laurence, Mordecai Richler and other bestselling Canadian novelists write trash?"

Jones and her principal looked at each other, then warily at me. "Well, I've certainly heard of Margaret Laurence and her book, the...?" said the principal.

"*Diviners*," Jones filled in. "But I've never personally read those books either."

"I was telling our guest we'd be interested in getting a list from her of Canadian books for our library," Breitkreutz said breezily.

"Of course the ones you mentioned we will consider," stressed Jones, "but you understand a committee here at the school has to read them and approve them before they go on the shelves."

I asked her if she was planning to ask for special dispensation from the Alberta government, so Millwoods would not have to comply with the guidelines for Canadian content in English literature.

She hesitated. "I hope it won't come to that. But if I as a member of staff can't find the proper type of book for our spiritual and moral values, we won't have much choice."

Proudly she told me she had read most of the books in the school library, and approved all of them. Even these? I asked. I showed her one of eight copies of *None Dare Call It Conspiracy—The Inside Story of the Rockefellers* by Gary Allen. Allen's book details the lives and careers of prominent Americans including Richard Nixon, the Kennedys, John Kenneth Galbraith and Henry Kissinger and demonstrates how they are not only slaves to socialism but also part of a huge conspiracy organized by Communists to take over the United States. The book would have one believe that every government measure from graduated income tax to public schools is part of the conspiracy.

I asked librarian Jones why the book was on the shelf.

"I don't know. I haven't read it yet."

I told her that I had read it and that it was full of distortions and even smacked of anti-Semitism—especially when Allen reports that Jews control international banking networks which have clearly "bankrolled the Russian Revolution."

Jones was stymied when I asked her how the book could have gotten into the school library, since she had never approved it.

I suggested the school might have received the books the way I had, free from the John Birch Society.

Jones and Breitkreutz were silent. Then Jones piped up, "Well, you have your opinion and we have ours, that's all there is to it!"

But I persisted. I noticed all the books in the library were classified according to the Dewey system, and that there were no books in the 300s, 400s, or 500s. In fact the subjects of the books jumped from the 200s (Bible prophecy) to mechanics in the 600s. I asked why sociology, psychology and political science were missing from their collection.

Jones was blunt and a bit impatient. "Most of sociology and psychology is just secular humanism. They provide a man-centred answer rather than a God-centred one like in the Bible. Those books tell students to rebel. Our students don't need to read those types of books. We want our students to approach authority in the proper way. We teach the children that to rebel against their parents is to rebel against God."

Lunchtime was nearly over and Breitkreutz broadly hinted I would be more an intruder than a guest at the afternoon Bible Study groups. Just before I left, Jones managed a smile and a parting pat on the arm.

"You know, I used to be just like you. I went to university and was filled with all those ideas about secular humanism. But I became a born again at the age of 24 when I started teaching and I saw there was only one way—God's way."

# 12

# A Day at Huntley Street

"Your name, please?" asked Diane Alimena, front desk receptionist at the 100 Huntley Street headquarters and television studio in downtown Toronto. I recognized the sparkling eyes and dark good looks. A very photogenic member of the 100 Huntley Street singers, she had graced one cover of the ministry's monthly magazine and Bible Study guide, *New Directions.*

"Of course I remember you from Washington for Jesus." She was friendly. "Just go right through these doors and into the cafeteria. You don't have to be in the studio till 8:45."

It was three days before Christmas, and I was part of the studio audience of the only Canadian daily Christian television show, 100 Huntley Street.

The studio and the ministry occupy a two-storey, 1954 vintage red-brick building in downtown Toronto at 100 Huntley Street, down the street from the CTV offices and several blocks from CBC headquarters. The building is the former recreation centre for the Confederation Life Insurance Company which leased it at an "extremely reasonable" figure to the ministry till the year 2002. (But David Mainse confidently says they won't need it till then; he expects the Lord to return long before then.) Rev. David Mainse is host of the television show and president of Crossroads Christian Communications, Inc., a registered Canadian charitable organization, which produces a dozen Christian TV programmes each week in six languages, not counting English, and a weekly show in sign language for the deaf. In his autobiography, *100 Huntley Street*, he writes, "Confederation Life had thought they were building a recreation centre, but God knew they were building a television studio. Hallelujah!"

100 Huntley Street first went on air June 15, 1977. The preceding November, Mainse made a pilgrimage to the U.S. to see Pat Robertson, host of Christian Broadcasting Network's 700 Club, and Jim Bakker of The PTL Club. "Nothing would be more foolish, not to say wasteful of God's money, than to try to duplicate what they were already doing. So if either of them was planning to come into Canada, then instead of starting a programme myself, I intended to offer my services to help them in any way I could, opening doors for them or acting as one of their Canadian representatives, whatever they wanted," explains Mainse in his book. "They assured me that they were not going to come into Canada, especially in the wake of recent legislation requiring of Canadian television stations that at least 60 percent of their programming be of Canadian origin."

When Mainse found that the new Global network did not have adequate production facilities for a 90-minute daily show featuring music, guests and a bank of telephone counsellors, he set out to build his own production studio from scratch.

He was able to parlay his TV success with a local show called "Crossroads" in Sudbury and Hamilton and his lease into a very favourable million-dollar financing package from RCA and friends in the banking community. He was ready to ride the crest of the wave of television evangelism that was about to sweep North America.

That was in October 1976. Six months later, both American evangelists had set up Canadian operations, despite their assurances to Mainse.

They had obviously revised their estimation of the market in their neighbour to the north. Today, The 700 Club has a small Canadian head office in Don Mills, Ontario. Two people work full-time in the financial planning department, two in the office and two more edit the 90-minute daily shows taped at the Virginia Beach headquarters down into half-hour segments aired three times each day in the Toronto area, once on Global (8:30 a.m.), and twice on Channel 47 (multilingual TV).

"But the best time to watch is from 1:00 to 2:30 p.m. weekdays," explains Gail Heron of the Canadian office. "You get to see the entire show which was live from Virginia Beach at 10:00 a.m. the same day."

Today the Christian Broadcasting Associates (the Canadian office) spends over $1.5 million each year, buying air time on undoubtedly grateful Canadian TV stations. All donations that come in to the Canadian box number are receipted in the Canadian office. It's quite a job. Money sent to the Canadian box is used exclusively in Canada, insists Heron—unless the donor specifically requests it be used for another mission—like a donation the the new CBN-TV station in Israel for instance. The only special mission to Canadian viewers is a counselling service. Over 80 Canadian volunteers man the phone lines in Toronto 24 hours a day, handling prayer requests from the local phone number that crawls along the bottom of the screen.

The PTL Club also has an office in Canada, but Jim Bakker's Canadian empire is just a shadow of its once-glorious past. Four years after its first broadcast in Canada, after pressure from Canadian supporters, Jim Bakker finally came to visit. In November 1981, The PTL Club put on a gigantic show at the Harbour Castle Hilton on Toronto's waterfront which featured Bakker. But his promise to return to Toronto every year has not been kept. In fact, he's never been back.

The five Canadian members of the PTL Board (Bakker was the sixth) had voted to spend any donations, over and above the cost of purchasing Canadian air time, to establish a religious retreat for Canadian born agains called Harvest Village, near Orangeville, Ontario.

Former Canadian president Stan Tufford believed the idea was a good one, "After all, the American PTL has its Heritage U.S.A. in South Carolina—but how many Canadians can afford to go there?" he asked.

But Bakker was adamant. He demanded all the money, over and above Canadian operating expenses, be returned to head office in Charlotte, North Carolina. "They are always building down there," observed Tufford. "They never get even one building paid for before they start another. They want to keep control over the Canadian operations. If that's the way they wanted to operate—I didn't want anything to do with PTL—even if we did help build them in Canada."

The entire Canadian board resigned over the dispute which left bitter feelings. "Without my faith in the Lord I would have asked 'what gives?' much earlier," says Tufford.

It was a race to the bank; the U.S. organization grabbed all the money, and Tufford started the retreat on his own resources. "All I have to say is it's time Canadians started taking a second look at what the Americans do with our money." According to another Canadian supporter, taking the matter to court would have just "hurt the work of the Lord."

Today, The PTL Club Television Network of Canada is housed in a small office in the Skyline Hotel, near the Toronto airport. With only four employees, most of their time is spent "processing donations," explained a staff member who identified herself as "Esther." "Right now there is no counselling service available, but we're looking into it."

She says the donations stay in Canada to pay for air time and running the office. The PTL Club is carried by Toronto's Multilingual Channel 47, seven days a week for an hour in the early morning and another hour at midnight. If people call for prayer or advice during office hours (a Canadian address and phone number are provided at the end of the broadcast along with their U.S. counterparts) the staff fields the calls. Anyone who can't be handled over the phone is referred to a local pastor or 100 Huntley Street for counselling.

The PTL Club is now just another American outfit with a Canadian distribution set up. The man in charge is John Franklin, an American from head office in Charlotte, who visits the Toronto branch office once or twice a month to make sure everything is running smoothly.

The third TV evangelist frontrunner, Jerry Falwell, has no Canadian phone number, just a box in Richmond Hill. He's seen in the Toronto area only on Sundays.

Lanny Morey, senior programme analyst at the Canadian Radio-television and Telecommunications Commission in Ottawa, says that a lot of people complained that American evangelical crusades into Canadians' living rooms and into their pocket books were just short of obscene. Morey admits the committed think it's wonderful, and that the prevailing liberal attitude is "who are we to condemn them?"

Can the government regulate the U.S.-based telecasts and fundraising appeals?

"The CRTC has no jurisdiction to regulate fundraising appeals. Indeed, I was told some of these ministries go to people on their deathbeds and get the money 'for Jesus' so it won't go to probate."

When Major B. F. Chaney appeared at the CRTC public hearings on religious broadcasting in January 1982, he warned about the dangers of the evangelists' television fundraising techniques. He cited the case of his own mother, an elderly widow living in Kentville, Nova Scotia, who was going broke giving all her money to the Rex Humbard crusade. After she was interviewed on CBC-TV's Fifth Estate, she received three calls from Humbard asking her to publicly retract her statements. When she refused, she was verbally abused and threatened with being barred from heaven.

For private networks, such as Global TV in Ontario, ITV in Alberta, or Multilingual TV in Toronto, 60 percent of their total broadcast package, averaged over a year, must be Canadian. In the prime-time hours of 6:00 to 12:00 p.m., that figure may drop to 50 percent.

Only the CBC must keep to a 60 percent Canadian quota at all times. The CBC is not permitted advocacy programming.

Morey explains, "A show like 100 Huntley Street, which is produced in Toronto and is mostly Canadian in content and has mainly Canadian guests and performers, actually helps Canadian broadcasters qualify for their Canadian content requirement."

Global gets the best of both worlds. Not only does it run Canadian content and score points with the CRTC, but 100 Huntley Street pays the network to do it. Original Canadian programming usually *costs* the network's money, most often far more than the revenue it generates through commercials. On religious programming alone, Global TV is said to have billed in excess of $2 million in 1981. Other stations take between one-half and one million dollars every year.

100 Huntley Street reportedly pays over $1500 per hour of broadcast time to Global TV, for example. For six years, 100 Huntley Street bought one and a half hours daily (including Sunday in some places) on Global. In 1979, Huntley Street expanded into the area of Christian Multilingual Programming (CMP) with eight one-hour and half-hour weekly shows in seven languages; it also produced Soul Set Free, a show "for and by the black community"—for which it has had to buy more air time on Toronto's Multilingual Channel 47. Add to that their half-hour programmes such as the still sporadic documentary series, Crossroads ("confronting key social issues of the 1980s"), Circle Square for children, and

Signs of the Times for the deaf—and the total weekly purchase of air time is around 16 hours. It costs a lot, but it must pay.

"Nothing's free," states Faithe Frew, advertising coordinator for 100 Huntley Street. "It used to be that some religious programming was given a 15-minute slot after the news or early in the mornings for free. Not any more. For 100 Huntley Street we pay for every hour we're on the air."

Morey thinks 100 Huntley Street may have actually brought paying for broadcast time on themselves. "In 1965, no religious programmes in Canada had to pay for TV time," she explains. "In 1977, 29 percent of Canadian religious programmes were paid time but today, 93 percent pay for their time. When 100 Huntley Street started the trend of paying for TV time it started the move away from local religious broadcasting into national big-time television."

But the recession hit Mainse and his rapidly expanding empire hard. "I've never written a letter like this before. This is the most urgent one ever!" was printed in blue scrawl across the top of Mainse's May 5, 1982 letter to his "faith partners." "What can I say except that I feel a great love for you," it continued, underlined in blue. "You have been the great extension of God's loving heart to this Ministry. Now I must come to you again." What followed was a fundraising pitch to save the ministry.

"Important" was handwritten in script.

Typed but underlined in blue, "I believe that a still, small voice tells me now that unusually large amounts (as far as regular giving patterns are concerned) will be given and that the Holy Spirit will be faithful to speak to everyone who receives this."

Apparently it failed and so, in June 1982, 100 Huntley Street rolled back the daily telecast from 90 to 60 minutes and cut down foreign-language productions to those six, including French, "from which God gives the greatest results." Administrative overhead was cut to the bare bones and senior staff accepted a 10 percent pay cut. The Bible Study Guide, *New Direction*, dropped its glossy four-colour format temporarily and began appearing mostly in black and white.

Still, the money rolls in. When Prey-TV, a U.S. docu-drama critical of the power of the televangelist ministries, was aired, over 25,000 people jammed the phone lines trying to get through to the fictitious prayer hotline as the number slid along the bottom of the TV screen, as it does on Huntley Street. And that was just make-believe.

Who are the big takers on the evangelical TV shows in Canada?

In 1981, according to the tax returns on non-profit organizations on file in Ottawa and available to the public, 100 Huntley Street received $7,600,000 in donations from viewers. Second to it was the American Christian tycoon of TV and radio, Herbert W. Armstrong, publisher of *The Plain Truth* magazine, with his The World Tomorrow broadcasts on Channel 3 and numerous U.S. stations that broadcast into the Toronto area, which took in $7,4000,000. After him was another American, Rex Humbard, who collected a neat $4,000,000 from Canadians.

Can they take their money and run?

"Absolutely," said Morey. "They promise to spend the money in Canada, on their Canadian ministries, but the government demands no receipts to show how that money is spent. As an example I once saw a return from Jerry Falwell's Old Time Gospel Hour. Falwell or someone on his staff had written 'not applicable' across it."

Faithe Frew is a calm, level-headed woman at 100 Huntley Street who has her fingers on the pulse of religious broadcasting.

"The average quarter-hour cumulative viewing audience—that is the number of people across Canada who have tuned into their television for a given quarter hour—on Sunday mornings is 2,591,600. And all of them are watching religious programming—whether it's our show, Meeting Place or the People's Church. I wonder if the mainline churches' attendance at that time equals that figure?

"People need to find the honest message and they seem to find it in smaller churches where there is fellowship and Bible Study during the week as well as on Sundays," she explained.

In four and a half years, the volunteers at the 25 counselling centres which Huntley Street runs across Canada and in the U.S. have handled over 750,000 calls. Most are from people with family problems, from potential suicides or from people who want to praise the Lord and give prayers of thanks. What do the Huntley Street counsellors do for these people?

Frew explains, "We ask people over the air to go to their phones and tell us when they are touched by God. After they commit their lives, we try to get them into churches or we notify their local pastor about them. Usually, they get involved in prayer groups or Bible Study sessions or Devotions during the week. Some people do some hospital visiting. We can only do so much on the phone anyway."

Though Huntley Street has never run a donor profile, Frew sums up who watches, who phones and who probably contributes financially to the ministry. "The majority of our viewing audience is over 50 years of age and female. But whenever we run a prime-time special [on Global TV—Sunday nights between ten and eleven] we see a tremendous number of salvations spanning all ages."

The Huntley Street cafeteria is a crescent-shaped room on the main floor, painted an institutional salmon-pink with cream trim. As it was Christmastime, the walls had been brightened by lime-green plastic holly, tinsel and snowflakes suspended from the light fixtures. Tin foil streamers decked the window. There were a few rows of wooden tables, end-to-end, dormitory style, and numerous round tables which seated eight. The cloth-covered armchairs were threadbare but serviceable.

I looked around the room for a place to sit and for a familiar, or at least a friendly, face. Most of the 30 people who had come to be part of the audience that day were women. Some sat in clusters of two or three, chatting away; others sipped their coffees alone hoping another stranger would join them.

"Have a coffee on us," urged a tall, thin studio hostess with shoulder-length, tightly permed, red hair. She was smartly turned out in a tailored royal blue suit with a white blouse, oversized gold hoop earrings and stiletto heels. Her makeup was heavy but impeccable. She served me coffee in a shallow cup and cracked saucer.

I sat down at a table with a middle-aged man in tortoise-shell glasses. I tried to catch his eye and smile, but he shyly looked away, blinked back a tear and shifted as though he wanted to get up. Suddenly, another blue-suited, younger woman rushed over to him. Her long hair bounced on her shirt collar and her round face was solicitous. "Oh, Mr. Poynter," she gushed. "I'm so happy to see you here. You must be feeling better."

No reply.

But she didn't seem to notice. She patted his folded hands kindly. "I hope you like the way we're doing things now. I'll see you after the show. And, hey, Praise the Lord!" She almost saluted.

He smiled weakly, said nothing, and continued to drink his coffee. Jim Poynter and his wife Marian are longtime friends of Mainse. Until his illness he had been responsible for selecting and training volunteer telephone counsellors.

Before I had a chance to try some small talk, a man—about 30, with downy blonde hair, a beer belly and a plaid sports jacket—bounded onto the small stage at the front of the cafeteria.

"Hi there! My name is Bill Mustard, and I work here at 100 Huntley Street. It's swell to see all you folks join us today. Who here is from outside the Toronto area?" The standard audience warm-up was underway.

A few hands went up.

"Edmonton," yelled one man.

"Guelph."

"On every show, we get people from further away than that," Mustard cajoled. "There's *got* to be someone from the States here."

An attractive couple in their 30s waved their hands. "We're from Los Angeles, California."

"Praise the Lord," said Mustard, "from all that way. What brought you up HERE at *this* time of year? *We* usually go down there."

He strained to hear their answer above the tinny sound of Christmas carols piped into the room. "Oh," he repeated for our benefit, "so you folks are here to get married on Christmas Eve—isn't that nice!"

A few people mumbled, "Praise the Lord."

"I just got a note from our hostess, Iva May. She says there is a family here from Ventura, California! Now *that's* farther than L.A., isn't it?"

One person applauded. Mustard continued.

"I should know the distance down there. I'm an American myself! Anyway, today we have a great show for you. We have our own Huntley Street singers; we have our own Father Bob MacDougall and much more.

. ."But first a few little hints that will help *us* and help *you* enjoy your day here. He whipped a list out of his pocket and smiled.

"Please follow exactly what Iva May tells you. She knows what to do during the telecast. When we ask you to applaud, don't do it half-heartedly. Do it as if God's depending on it —which He is.

"If you have to go to the washroom, wait until the lights are off the studio audience. Raise your hand and Iva May will be sure to get you on and off camera fast.

"If you've got dark glasses on or those kind that turn dark in bright lights, please take them off when the lights go up, otherwise you'll look like a shady character."

A little giggling from the audience.

"We've got a whole day of activities planned just for you. First, let's finish off our coffees and put the cups on that table over there.

"Now, after the show is over, at about 11:00, there is individual prayer and counselling in the chapel for anyone who has anything to get off his chest or any special requests to make of the Lord.

"The rest of you can visit our bookstore and pick up some last minute gifts for Christmas.

"Don't forget our Huntley Street mugs—$4.50—for that extra something in the stocking! Lunch will be served from 11:30 to 12:30 right here. The food's good," he patted his paunch, "and the price is right."

A few guffaws from the man in the chef's uniform behind the counter.

"After that there is Bible Study and then a tour of the studio and you can see how we produce Huntley Street and our other shows like Circle Square and Inside Track [now defunct]. Now, how does that sound? A whole day of events just for you."

No response.

Undaunted he went on. "Now we have someone here from our still photography department who is going to come into the studio with us and take our picture. You can get a souvenir of your day at Huntley Street for only $3. The pictures will be ready in the cafeteria right after the show and I hope you'll all order one."

Iva May lined us up in twos to go into the studio across the hall. I was stationed beside a 40-year-old woman and her five-year-old daughter. "I come here quite often," she said.

"This is my last child at home and I have more time on my hands."

Iva May sat the engaged couple from L.A. in the front row of the bleachers. The woman and little girl were put in the empty set of bleachers beside the ones where the rest of us sat in case the child had to go to the washroom more than once.

Fifteen feet away from the bleachers was the set. There were four hopsack-covered armchairs around a teakwood coffee table. Plastic holly and tinsel were wired to the orange-curtained backdrop. A replica of the nativity scene sat on the coffee table.

David Mainse, radiant, smiling, bursting out of his buttoned suit jacket, strode toward us, arms outstretched. The stage manager yelled two more minutes to air.

Mainse thanked us for coming, and told us Huntley Street couldn't exist without us. Iva May pointed out the couple soon to be married and he shook their hands.

He turned to the rest of us earnestly. "Now our photographer is gonna take a picture of us here, and Father Bob and I will join you for the picture. You will have to pay $3 for each one because we don't want to spend *one cent* of you donation to TV evangelism for this photo service."

Two directors' chairs were pulled to the front of the bleachers. Mainse and Father Bob—a charismatic who once studied for the Jesuit priesthood, and who dresses in street clothes—sat down. All of a sudden Mainse shouted out, "Who's your Lord and Saviour?"

"Jesus," shot back the studio audience just as the shutter clicked.

The house lights went down and spotlights highlighted the living room part of the set. A softer light formed a pool on a small platform a few feet from set where two young men and two younger women stood, microphones in hand. One of them was Mainse's daughter. Elaine Stacey, at 23, is one half of the most popular Canadian born-again musical duo. Her husband, Bruce Stacey, is also the manager of Mainroads Productions, part of Huntley Street's Crossroads

Christian Communications, Inc., which produces records and tapes featuring artists who appear on the television show.

Elaine started to sing and the Huntley Singers joined in:

*He's the reason for the season,*
*He's the purpose of it all,*
*He's the God of our Creation and the mighty Lord of all;*
*He's the reason for the season,*
*For the trimmings and the tree,*
*May this Christmas time remind you that He came to set*
*    man free.*

Half-way through the refrain, the white telephones started ringing softly at the 18 prayer-counsellor desks which are banked at the side of the set. As each telephone buzzed, one counsellor's face after another lit up. They became animated, cradling the receiver with their shoulders, pen in one hand, other outstretched. They closed their eyes as they prayed with the person at the other end of the line. The Huntley Street counsellors are volunteers who go through training at the ministry so they can field questions, offer prayers and sympathy and get the names and addresses of prospective faith partners. All of them wear little blue name tags; some look like young housewives who spend a couple of mornings a week at the studio, others could be pensioners. Signs in the halls and the cafeteria advertised for volunteer counsellors.

In front of each counsellor was a looseleaf book in which she wrote the name of the person who called for help, the particular request and, if the caller was willing, his or her address and telephone number.

As the camera panned the bank of counsellors, the man I sat beside in the cafeteria stood at his desk and waved.

"That's Jim Poynter, a staff member here at Huntley Street who has been off sick for six months," Mainse's voice

On the set of 100 Huntley Street. In the foreground is Father Bob (*left*) and David Mainse. Directly behind Father Bob is the couple about to be married. Judith Haiven is in the second-last row, third from the left.

*Top*: Egbert and Gert are regulars on Circle Square, the Huntley empire's children's show. *Below*: The "Salute to Canada" prayer meeting, Varsity Stadium, Toronto.

boomed. "It's nice to see you back again, hard at work, helping people, Jim." While the show broke for an advertisement for their prime-time Christmas special, Mainse told Jim he did very well. "Don't worry, we wouldn't ask you to say anything on the air."

Iva May whispered to us that Jim had had a stroke and though he couldn't talk, he could sing "like a canary." Right after the ad, Mainse told the viewers, "We really have a treat for you today. Jim Poynter who is just recovering from a stroke is going to sing Silent Night for us." Without any accompaniment, Jim sang the tune in a wobbly and high-pitched voice. He didn't miss a word.

"Praise the Lord," Mainse said warmly afterward.

"God certainly works in strange ways," whispered a young girl beside me. "What a blessing."

Mainse held a stack of papers up to the camera. "Do you know what these are?" he smiled. "Here are 483 petition forms with 2188 names for the CRTC. Now our American viewers won't know what we're talking about, nor will some of you who just tuned in.

"But the Canadian Radio-television and Telecommunications Commission, Canada's broadcasting regulatory body, is holding hearings on religious broadcasting in Ottawa on January 26 [1982]. We pray that those hearings will pave the way for us to apply for a license so we can operate a satellite channel here in Canada. We'd like to present programmes for children and teenagers, news shows and documentaries. But buying air time every day gets very expensive.

"So whether you go around to your neighbours or stand in a shopping mall and ask people to sign our petition, *please* get them filled in and mailed to us postmarked before December 31."

Lanny Morey at the CRTC in Ottawa told me the petitions never came through. "They aimed for a million signatures and they promised to dump bags of mail on us but they never did. They never even presented their petition at the hearings. And David Mainse never personally appeared." However, fellow evangelist Bill Prankard and his wife Gwen, whose show appears on CJOH and Global (both in Ottawa), did file letters on Huntley's behalf, from viewers, written on the back of preprinted donation envelopes. Many of these letters contained lurid testimonies of diseases and family tragedies, all endured with the help of their shows.

Mainse's co-host that December day was Father Bob MacDougall, who used to practise as a clinical psychologist. Mainse reported that a viewer's letter indicated he was hearing voices. "Could that be so scientifically?" Mainse asked MacDougall.

MacDougall called the phenomenon "audio schizophrenia": "It's like when Mary heard the word of the Lord and she experienced that inner peace. There are three sources of audio schizophrenia," he added. "The first source is God, just as he talked to Mary that time. The second source could be a chemical imbalance in certain people which allows them to hear voices. The third source is a demon, the voice of Satan. In my years as a clinical psychologist I've seen oppressive darkness come upon people in many ways. We must tighten our hold over satanic spirits in the name of God." I felt chilly.

Mainse came back, "But you'd advise a person who thought he or she had heard a voice to consult a doctor, wouldn't you?"

"A doctor *and* a pastor," MacDougall chided. (Father MacDougall has since left the show for pastoral work in Nova Scotia.)

The first guest that morning was David Johnston, a

minister from the Pentecostal Assemblies of Canada. A slim man with a salt-and-pepper beard, he wore a creased brown leisure suit and carried a pocket-sized copy of the New Testament.

"I'm just a little scared of making a blooper," Johnston apologized to Mainse.

Mainse laughed. "At the Huntley Street Christmas party, the crew showed clips from programmes where guests or the staff made gaffes. Since this show goes live to air, there's no chance to mend anything people say. Sometimes it's hilarious!"

Johnston started his testimony with a joke. "Know why I have this beard? I asked my wife one day if I could grow one. She said, 'Yes, as long as it will improve your appearance!'" Embarrassed silence.

"So I got back at her. She came home from the beauty parlour one day and I told her she didn't look any different than before she went," he chuckled. No one else did.

Mainse glared at him; Johnston got back on track. "You and Father Bob were talking about hearing the Lord just a while ago. But how do you *know* if you hear the Lord or not? If the voice isn't tranquil and gentle, it's not the voice of the Lord," he said sagely.

"Some people don't trust young folks today. But Jesus' disciples, John and Paul, were just teenagers when they walked with the Lord. And they were rebels. Today they probably would have worn leather, chains and swastikas!"

No audience reaction. Mainse shuffled his petitions nervously and went on to introduce Mrs. Pansy Hart, a Kitchener, Ontario housewife who had found the Lord. Pansy sat in her powder blue pleated dress, ankles delicately crossed and a large family Bible in her lap.

"I had two nervous breakdowns," she began. "After the second one I accepted the Lord, and decided I'd follow Him. Before that, my marriage was full of arguments, bitterness and drinking and smoking. I smoked up to four packages of cigarettes a day. I lived on tranquillizers. I had married

young, at 17. Though I grew up in a Pentecostal home, my
husband didn't know the Lord, nor did I those first 13 years
of marriage.

"I can't fault my mother, because she encouraged me to
send my three children to religious school.

"I used to care for a foster baby some time ago. He came to
us when he was only seven days old. After only five weeks,
he died of crib death. From that day on I decided to live my
life for the Lord.

"I changed quite a lot. I was calmer and didn't fight at all
with my husband. Finally one day he asked me what had
changed me. After I told him, he told me he wanted to share
Christ with me. So the next Sunday he came with me to
church and accepted the Lord. He's given me the ability to
write poetry." She read a poem which praised the Lord.

"Isn't that wonderful?" Mainse was glowing. "I see your
husband and wonderful children in the audience today." He
waved and the camera dollied up to the bleachers and zeroed
in on four smiling faces in the first row.

"That's right, David," beamed Pansy, "and I tell my
daughter who is now 17 to remember to follow the way of
the Lord."

"Amen," said Mainse.


"Our next guest needs no real introduction," said Mainse.
"Perhaps you people know the Italian version of 100 Huntley
Street is shown in Italy and we Canadians don't have to pay a
cent for it! The Italian people pay for the air time and all we
do is ship over the tapes. Isn't that wonderful? Our next guest
is Tom Grazziola, the producer of *Vive Cento Per Cento*—or
100 Percent Living, in Italian."

"Merry Kinosis, David," smiled Grazziola.

"Don't you mean Merry Christmas?"

"No, Merry Kinosis." Grazziola held up a large edition of
the *Good News Bible*. "It says in here that Christmas was a

declaration of war. It was the first phase of a planned invasion of the earth by our Lord. The demons trembled when they heard this cry, David. What the Scriptures called for was the liberation of Planet Earth by an ICBM."

"An inter-continental ballistic missile?" asked Mainse.

Grazziola laughed. "Of course not. An inter-celestial blessing missile—an ICBM. You see, David, the Baby in Bethlehem is coming back and He's coming back with a shout. But this time it's not a miracle."

"Praise the Lord."

"Now I want all you people in the studio audience to stand up," Mainse exhorted. "I bet you didn't think you'd have a chance to perform on live television today! Let's sing some praise to the Lord. 'O come all ye faithful, joyful and triumphant...'"

The camera dollied toward us, so I stood up and sang along with the rest of the crowd.

I hoped my husband was watching.

Right after the show, Mainse came over to the stand and reviewed his troops. "You did a wonderful job today. I want to thank you all for coming. This programme wouldn't be possible without all the help we get from people like you. Father Bob, any Good News from the prayer counsellors?"

"There certainly is, David! One woman, down to her last cent, out of work, with a family to feed, called in to accept Christ. Another woman, who had called in for more information on the ministry a few weeks ago, called back today and opened her heart to Jesus," MacDougall read from the counsellors' report sheets.

"Well, well. That is the aim of our ministry, and I can see from all the calls we got today how many new people we are helping know the Lord," Mainse enthused. "But this ministry costs money. It is expensive to buy air time, expensive to have studios like these. You know, some people say to me,

'David, why do you need studios as large and well-equipped as your neighbours like the CBC and CTV down the street?' I say, nothing is too good for carrying on the Lord's work, isn't that right?"

Without a cue from the stage manager and without the lights going up, the audience clapped loudly. The taping was over.

"Well, I understood the photos from earlier today are ready to be picked up. Makes a nice souvenir," said Mainse. "And Iva May is going to hand out these little envelopes for your donations. If you're already a partner of 100 Huntley Street, please check that box. If you're not, we'll send you a free trial subscription to our *New Direction* magazine. Did anyone forget their cheque book?"

A couple of hands went up.

"Don't worry. There is a counter-cheque on the flap of the envelope; just fill it in."

My neighbour glared as I quickly put two dollar bills into the envelope. She busily filled in the blank cheque.

"Individual prayer counselling this way, lunch is straight ahead," Iva May directed us out of the studio.

One older woman in a cranberry dress and matching pillbox hat hobbled beside Iva May. "Can I talk to David?" she asked boldly.

Iva May put her hand on the woman's arm and steered her to the individual prayer counselling room. "No," said the woman firmly. "I want to speak to David."

Mainse must have heard her and came over. She stammered: "I just...wanted...to say, I love this show," the woman said haltingly. "And...I've been alone since 1964, when my sister...died. Alone every Christmas. It's hard, but being here helps." She was crying.

Mainse asked, "You are *alone* every Christmas?"

The woman nodded.

"Well this year we just won't let you be alone. What is your name, dear? I want you to join my family and me for Christmas at our house. How would you like that?"

"Do you mean it?" She stared in disbelief.

"I certainly do. We'd be delighted to have you."

Twenty of us filed into the small chapel behind the cafeteria for our individual prayer counselling session. Father Bob MacDougall was in charge, and three young men on staff at Huntley Street were there to help out.

MacDougall is a leprechaun of a man with piercing brown eyes, a ruddy complexion, and an ever-smiling mouth. "It's wonderful to see all you people coming in for prayer and fellowship. I've seen most of you before at Huntley Street, haven't I?" he enthused, studying the faces before him.

The kitchen-type chairs were pushed back to the perimeter of the chapel, and we stood in little clusters before him. There was no podium, no chancel—no religious object in the room. "Let's get a little closer together," he commanded, "and let's really praise the Lord!"

"I know a person here has some troubles at home, some weighty problems. Perhaps a son who is taking drugs or a daughter failing in school..."

A squawk of recognition came from a bulky middle-aged woman ahead of me.

Father Bob closed his eyes and swayed as he spoke. "Another person here has an incurable disease...what is it now? Oh yes, multiple sclerosis. And you are worried. But let God take that worry out of your heart; trust Him for the answers to all of your problems. Some people here don't seem to have enough faith to get them through. Lord Jesus, please nurture their faith and allow them to let You into their hearts..."

The tall awkward young man beside me held up his hands. "Does anyone have anything they want to get off their chests? Let God show you the way," coaxed Father Bob. "I want you all to hold hands with the person next to you—whether you know him or not. Let His spirit fill you. Tell the person beside you your problems, your fears."

The young man held one of my hands, and a woman who looked like his mother held my other hand, and gently asked if there was anything I'd like to confess. There were tears in the woman's eyes. I murmured no. So the young man and the woman hugged each other and muttered a litany of words and phrases.

I jumped when Father Bob's hands rested on my shoulders. "I want to know, have you accepted Christ as your personal Saviour?"

"No, not yet."

He drifted toward an Italian woman in a wheelchair. Her friend translated his question for her. She nodded and held up her hands.

"Who here needs a miracle—come right up here," Father Bob commanded. Ten believers formed a circle around him. Behind them were the three young men from the ministry.

The pretty Los Angeles fiancee went first. Father Bob put his hands on her shoulders, muttered something about the Lord and pushed her backward, hard. Her fiance caught her under her arms as she fell back. "When you let go, God takes over! Hallelujah," Father Bob rejoiced.

The prospective groom cushioned the fall of his bride and eased her down onto the carpet. Her eyes were closed and there was an angelic smile on her lips as she lay stretched out at Father Bob's feet.

"Who's next?" he asked.

The housewife with the little girl left the daughter with the woman beside her and stepped forward. Father Bob slapped his hands on her shoulders, said a prayer and pushed her back, reminding her to let go so God could take over. She shrieked and fell straight back. The little daughter started to cry. Father Bob picked her up and asked her if she'd like to marry him. The child shook her head, stopped crying and stood beside her mother's prone body.

A woman stood up, put her Bible on the seat behind her and stood before Father Bob. Another prayer, a Praise the Lord! and a touch on the shoulders sent her backward. She was caught by a staff man and lay beside the mother, eyes tearing and body shaking with faith.

A skinny Black man raised his hand. Father Bob quietly counselled him for a minute, felt his forehead and gave him a gentle push. Someone helped him down to the floor where he lay, arms extended upwards. He kept on repeating "Praise the Lord" while Father Bob prayed with the others who remained standing. He urged them to yield to a new surge of God's love.

After ten minutes, the room was silent. Half a dozen people lay on the carpet. The others stood serenely with heads bowed, waiting for benediction.

"Well, what are you waiting for?" guffawed Father Bob, to break the tension. He stretched out a hand to the Black man on the carpet. "Let me help you up!"

# Afterword

I'm sure most writers—even experienced writers—will agree that writing a book is an emotionally draining experience. When the writing is over and you begin to see the book being produced (the neat typeset galleys, the first proof of the colour cover), there is relief—but mixed with a sense of anxiety. Did I do justice to the subject? Was I fair? On the other hand, was I too easy on people who didn't deserve it? Have I said what needed saying?

All these thoughts scrambled through my mind as the book was about to go to press. But more than this understandable nervousness, I was struck by another, deeper feeling. I approached the task of writing *Faith, Hope, No Charity* as an interesting assignment, but it had proved to be an exhausting and unsettling experience.

During the two years of research for the book, I found myself more and more deeply involved in the born-again world. Far from being simply a religious experience for the people I interviewed, their faith envelopes them like a steel cocoon. The following story, taken from *The Emerging Order* by Jeremy Rifkin, portrays a day in the life of a "Christian" family.

In the morning, husband and wife wake up to an evangelical service on their local Christian owned and operated radio station. The husband leaves for work where he will start off his day at a businessman's prayer breakfast. The evangelical wife bustles the children off to their Christian Day School. At midmorning she relaxes in front of the TV set and turns on her favorite Christian soap opera. Later in the afternoon, while the Christian husband is attending a Christian business seminar, and the children are engaged in an after-school Christian sports program, the Christian wife is doing her daily shopping at a Christian store, recommended in her Christian Business Directory. In the evening the Christian family watches the Christian World News on TV and then settles down for dinner. After dinner, the children begin their Christian school assignments. A Christian baby-sitter arrives—she is part of a baby-sitter pool from the local church. After changing into their evening clothes, the Christian wife applies a touch of Christian make-up, and then they're off to a Christian nightclub for some socializing with Christian friends from the local church. They return home later in the evening and catch the last half hour of the "700 Club," the evangelical Johnny Carson Show. The Christian wife ends her day reading a chapter or two from Marabel Morgan's best-selling Christian book, *The Total Woman*. Meanwhile her husband leafs through a copy of *Inspiration* magazine, the evangelical *Newsweek*, before they both retire for the evening.

When I first met Rifkin in 1980, his description seemed far-fetched. No longer. Researching and writing this book, I met many people whose lives were as circumscribed and narrow as Rifkin's imaginary family's. Add to this family picture a natural suspicion of anything different, throw in a knee-jerk reaction to "secular" authority and an equally automatic obedience to religious leaders, sprinkle with racial or religious intolerance, and you have a portrait of many of the people profiled in this book.

Getting to know them was not difficult. The non-famous, ordinary interviewees saw me as a possible new recruit and someone who could spread the word. The more famous born agains, the headliners, talked to me as any clever communicator uses the press. Most of the former were genuinely nice people, kind and helpful to strangers; most of the latter were courteous and willing to talk. Both were initially open—but only up to a very well-defined limit. As soon as it became clear that I was not convert-material or about to act the role of "impartial observer," their ingenuousness disappeared. This point usually came when they felt threatened or thought they were losing the argument or losing face with me. There may have been many reasons. Because the leaders are used to getting more than they give, I suspect their disinterest in me often arose when there was nothing more to be gained.

As a Jew who was raised in a liberal home, I was very disturbed by many born agains' refusal to understand or tolerate other religions or political viewpoints. Equally disturbing was their inability to find common cause with any political or social movement of a progressive nature or to identify with the disadvantaged. I was especially disturbed by their cynical, smothering "love" for the Jews, an affection based more on millenialist determinism than on genuine tolerance.

Many born-again Christians are blindly obliged to support the U.S. and its nuclear policies, necessary for our common defence against the Soviet "evil empire." According to them, the Book of Relevation warns that the end of the world—Armageddon—is coming. A nuclear holocaust will just be proof of God's Word in the Bible and nothing to fear. A few of Reagan's men, James Watt among them, have dismissed concern over long-range effects of government policies, saying that Biblical prophecies will likely intervene.

I do not want to tar all evangelists with the same brush. Many pursue their religion as a personal matter and believe that politics and religion are also personal matters for others.

Beyond that, there is a growing number of evangelical Christians who have a commitment to various forms of social activism and who will join in causes with others regardless of their religious beliefs. One notable example on the nuclear issue is well-known evangelist Billy Graham. In an interview on CBS television March 29, 1979, he deplored the "insanity and madness" of the heightening arms race. He is convinced that opposing all nuclear arms is "the teaching of the Bible." Since then, other moderate evangelical leaders have come out in opposition to nuclear proliferation. Rifkin notes: "It is quite possible that growing opposition to the nuclear arms race will provide many evangelicals with an entry point for a broader activist commitment to stewardship, just as the abolitionist cause did during...the nineteenth century."

However, it is difficult to escape the conclusion that the born-again leaders, particularly TV evangelists like Jerry Falwell, Pat Robertson, James Robison, Jim Bakker and Jimmy Swaggart, are, quite simply, dangerous men. Flip your television dial any Sunday morning from one televangelist to the next and you'll hear litanies of hatred and intolerance.

One recent Sunday morning I tuned into Jimmy Swaggart. Of all the TV evangelists, Swaggart, based in Baton Rouge, Louisiana, is the most charismatic and perhaps the most frightening. Where Falwell is big brother and Robertson is Dick Cavett, Swaggart, cousin of country-rock star Jerry-Lee Lewis, is all showman. As well as being arguably the most eloquent speaker, he plays piano and sings as well.

From any one else's mouth, his words would be mere cliches, spoken by a cartoon character. That day, preaching before a giant audience in Atlanta, Georgia, his impassioned denunciations were deadly serious. Trademark Bible in one hand, handkerchief in the other, Swaggart strode back and forth across the empty stage, shrieking, "I'm tired of liberal, communist fellow-travellers tearing down our country. I'm tired of pot-smoking and alcoholic ne'er-do-wells living on welfare. I'm tired of God-reviling 'secular humanists' telling us we can't have prayer in our schools."

The audience hung on every word, their heads nodding sagely whenever he made a point. They cheered and clapped when he talked of speaking to U.S. President Reagan on these very issues. Swaggart's message was crystal clear for all who cared to listen—suppress the undesirables who live in our country; subvert, overthrow and punish—even nuke them—if they live elsewhere. And the audience agreed with him 150 percent. I saw the same fervent certainty first-hand when I attended a Swaggart rally in Toronto's Massey Hall.

Evangelists like Swaggart are setting the spiritual pre-conditions for nuclear war. On his 1972 album *Sail Away*, musical satirist Randy Newman captured one facet of the rationale in his song "Political Science":

> No one likes us,
> I don't know why,
> We may not be perfect,
> But heaven knows we try,
> But all around,
> Even our old friends put us down,
> Let's drop the big one,
> And see what happens.
>
> We give them money,
> But are they grateful,
> No, they're spiteful,
> And they're hateful,
> They don't respect us,
> So let's surprise them,
> We'll drop the big one,
> And pulverize them.

But political paranoia is only one part of the rationale. Even the most rabid, non-religious cold-warrior has a profound respect for the destructive capacity of hydrogen bombs. But the millenialists insist that the coming war is part of God's plan. Nuclear holocaust is justified because it signifies Christ's return to rule the earth—or what's left of it. Combine these people with those who believe a nuclear war is "winnable" and you have a most dangerous chemistry.

This political phenomenon is of a new and different type in the annals of American politics. America's traditional imperialism of confidence is giving way to a post-Vietnam posture of fear and insecurity. U.S. imperialism has never been particularly benign or charitable, but in the past, and especially in the post-World War II years, it was the offspring of aggressive American liberalism. Catch-phrases like Roosevelt's "Good Neighbour Policy" and Kennedy's "Alliance for Progress" reflected the friendly big brother image the Americans had of themselves.

In his autobiography *Honorable Men*, former CIA director William Colby recalls his initial motivation to enter the Office of Strategic Services (the OSS, precursor to the CIA). A self-defined liberal, who once acted as an attorney for trade unions, Colby became a cold-warrior out of a sense of mission to spread America's "better way" to an under-developed world. A fervid anti-communism was mixed with a misguided pragmatism common in the Kennedy 60s, a belief that the United States had a duty to solve the world's problems. This overweening confidence in the American way gave rise, among many other catastrophes, to Colby's infamous "Phoenix Project," which cold-bloodedly assassinated tens of thousands of Vietnamese. To the well-known details of that war can be added countless instances of overt and covert operations to subvert governments and liberation movements all over the world. All of these brutal acts of counterinsurgency are despicable, but they seemed to occur in a geopolitical context which at least ruled out nuclear roulette. While doctrines of "massive deterrence" built a monstrous nuclear arsenal, the concept of "warfighting" was considered unthinkable. One never got the impression that these men were actually desirous of pushing the button. It is interesting that three of the top cold-warriors of the 50s and 60s, Colby, Robert McNamara and McGeorge Bundy, have recently come out strongly against present U.S. nuclear policy.

But now, after dishonourable defeat in Vietnam, after the oil crisis, after the U.S.'s economic battles with its trading partners and after the realization that its interests are opposed throughout the world, as recorded in the United Nations voting record, U.S. imperialism has changed. It is now an imperialism born of fear, of blind reaction, of paranoia and of righteous anger. And what is worse, for the first time you actually get the feeling that there are powerful men unafraid of nuclear war.

The born-again movement is one of the larger engines that drive this new train of thought in American politics. Richard A. Viguerie, a self-confessed "key figure in the New Right," explains the power of the TV evangelists and their followers in his book *The New Right: We're Ready to Lead*:

> Evangelists like Jerry Falwell, James Robison, and Pat Robertson, who reach over 20 million people by television every week, talked about political issues and urged their listeners to register to vote and get involved in politics.
> ...Jerry Falwell, for example, has formed the Moral Majority, Inc., an organization that aims to mobilize millions of Americans to work for pro-God, pro-family policies in government.
> The Moral Majority claims it registered 2.5 million voters and re-registered 1 to 1.5 million voters for the 1980 elections.
> ...Despite some efforts to belittle it, the Moral Majority lived up to its publicity. It and allied groups gave Ronald Reagan his margin of victory.

And Falwell is hard at work on 1984, according to Viguerie.

The foundation of the Moral Majority is fundamentalist Protestants, in particular the estimated 15 million Americans who watch Falwell's "Old Time Gospel Hour" regularly. Rev. Falwell has a remarkable base to work with. He already has 2 million names on his "Gospel Hour" mailing list.

But Dr. Falwell intends to build a coalition of not only his own religious followers but of Catholics, Jews and Mormons. . . . The potential of such a coalition is tremendous. There are an estimated 85 million Americans—50 million born-again Protestants, 30 million morally conservative Catholics, 3 million Mormons and 2 million Orthodox and Conservative Jews—with whom to build a pro-family, Bible-believing coalition.

Here Viguerie uses his friend Falwell to represent the nation-wide network of televangelists, political action groups and fundraising organizations which, together, make up the unique blend of old-right politics and new-style Christianity known as the New Right.

Of course, not all born agains are part of the New Right; many have little interest in party politics. But many are inducted into single-issue campaigns, whether the goal is tightening up on abortion laws, promoting prayer in the schools, or lobbying for public funding for private religious schools. Because nourishment for the soul is invariably mixed with a pitch for one right-wing cause or another, the laws of probability imply that the army of born agains is going to grow.

Is the born-again movement here to stay? The full answer to this question is complex, but there is reason to believe that as long as the economic situation of the 80s fails to improve, the instant and thoughtless panaceas of born-again Christianity will be seen as a vast sanctuary by millions of North Americans. Is this sanctuary really a recruitment camp for right-wing movements? It would be naive to think otherwise.

Can or should anything be done to protect people from the movement? The interview with Jean about her experiences at Teen Ranch is testimony to the fact that young people—especially school-age children—should be protected. But where do we in a supposedly democratic and pluralistic society draw the line? Whom do we protect? And if we impose censorship on these religious fundamentalists and their teachings, the same restrictions could be used against conscientious and socially active people who want to make our society more human

It is very easy to look at the trend of religious fundamentalism and think it represents the majority. The Moral Majority would certainly have us believe so. But in both the U.S. and Canada there is a strong liberal, free-thinking and, yes, humanist tradition. It forms the basis of the beliefs and values held by perhaps the real majority in both countries. It has found expression in the ongoing battle to expand our freedoms and to resist oppression; it marched in the civil rights movement and in the demonstrations that helped to stop the Vietnam war; today it decries U.S. involvement in Latin America and fights for social justice at the local and national levels and in the growing worldwide peace movement. Finally, there are the religious movements, deeply rooted in social activism, which have grown stronger and more visible during the period of born-again expansion. The hope for the future is not to muzzle the born-again movement, but for liberals, for humanists, to find a voice and to organize.

Our faith and hope may have been shaken by these ultra-conservative times, but the humanist movement still possesses one genuine virtue which the born-again New Right is unlikely ever to acquire—namely, the spirit of charity.

# Readings

Some of the books used in the preparation of *Faith, Hope, No Charity* are listed below for suggested reading. They are broken down into categories reflecting their general attitude toward the born-again phenomenon.

## Pro

Kienal, Paul A., *The Christian School: Why it is Right for Your Child*, Wheaton, Ill.: Victor Books, 1978.

Lindsey, Hal, *The Late Great Planet Earth*, Grand Rapids, Mich.: Zondervan, 1980.

Shaeffer, Franky, *A Time for Anger: The Myth of Neutrality*, Westchester, Ill.: Crossway Books, 1982.

Viguerie, Richard A., *The New Right: We're Ready to Lead*, Falls Church, Va., The Viguerie Company, 1981.

Webber, Robert E., *The Moral Majority: Right or Wrong?* Westchester, Ill.: Cornerstone Books, 1981.

## Con

Conway, Flo, and Siegelman, Jim, *Holy Terror: The Fundamentalist War on America's Freedoms in Religion, Politics and Our Private Lives*, Garden City, New York: Doubleday, 1982.

Dworkin, Andrea, *Right-Wing Women*, New York: Putnam's, 1983.

Hadden, Jeffrey K., and Swann, Charles E., *Prime Time Preachers: The Rising Power of Televangelism*, Reading, Mass.: Addison-Wesley, 1981.

Rifkin, Jeremy, with Ted Howard, *The Emerging Order: God in the Age of Scarcity*, New York: Putnam's, 1979.

Templeton, Charles, *The Third Temptation*, Toronto: McClelland and Stewart, 1980.

Vetter, Herbert F. (ed.), *Speak Out Against the New Right*, Boston: Beacon Press, 1982.

# Christians in the Nicaraguan Revolution

Margaret Randall

In *Christians in the Nicaraguan Revolution* Margaret Randall turns her attention to the country's Catholic Church and its remarkable transformation during the revolutionary period.

Her lengthy introduction reviews historical developments within the church and explains the important concept of *liberation theology*. Two sections are devoted to the conversations, or *testimonies*, of members of two Christian communities which participated in the 1979 revolution. The first community, Solentiname, was founded in the mid-1960s by Ernesto Cardenal, priest, poet and now minister of culture in the Nicaraguan government. The second, Riguero, is a Managua *barrio* community associated with Father Uriel Molina.

*"Brings home the key truth about political struggle in Central America: there has been no middle ground between revolution and the status quo."*
—Vancouver *Sun*

1983, 208 pp., illustrated, CIP
$ 7.95 paper ISBN 0-919573-15-0
$15.95 cloth ISBN 0-919573-14-2